For my wife, Li Li

YOUNG STEVE MCQUEEN

YOUNG STEVE MCQUEEN

SCREENPLAY BY **D.R.SCHOEL**

ISBN: 978-1-7773133-0-2

3RD WHEEL PRESS

All my life, I seemed always to be looking for something—never knowing what it was—but always there was the sense that I couldn't, and shouldn't, be confined.

Steve McQueen

CONTENTS

AUTHOR'S FOREWORD

Looking back on my computer files, I see that I started the first draft of this screenplay on May 18th, 2008. It's been a long road getting it to here, and quite a journey.

First, what about my connection to Steve McQueen: why did I choose to write this particular story? After all, I grew up in the eighties at a time when Steve had faded from the limelight; it was in the "old" days of channel hopping on cable TV—before Netflix—when I first discovered his films, and quite by accident. I believe the first movie I stumbled upon was The Magnificent Seven, either followed that day or the next (my memory is a little hazy) by the Great Escape. It might've been a retrospective on the History Channel.

I was transfixed. Who was this guy? I'd gone through film school without ever hearing about him. Humphrey Bogart, Lauren Bacall, Cary Grant, Katherine Hepburn... I'd heard about, but film teachers (and textbooks) never mentioned Steve. I did a quick search on *Yahoo*.

I soon learned that Steve's early life, before he became a star, was more fascinating and filled with adventure than any movie. As he's said, "I was like an old man by the time I was seventeen." I also found personal connections: there was mention of Steve finding his first love at Myrtle Beach in South Carolina. Myrtle Beach was a regular holiday destination for my family when I was growing up. At another point, Steve jumped ship in the Dominican Republic, another place I vacationed at when I was young. Steve served on Arctic exercises in Labrador, in my native country. I could literally *see* many of the locations he'd passed through.

In 2008, my first feature-film had been released, so I (somewhat presumptively) felt Steve's story would make a great follow-up. No one else seemed to be making a movie about his early life. To me, it seemed obvious.

I didn't know *then* where the writing of this screenplay would take me.

To be fair, in the beginning I struggled with it. That is, with shaping the material. I'd begun dating a beautiful Chinese girl, and I was still pretty high and conceited after my first theatrical release (not yet realizing how brutal life, and the film industry, could be). I shared that first draft of the script with her, and she read it—and told me it was garbage.

She was also interested in the arts and movies... and she was right. What followed were long conversations and after maybe half a year, the story began to shape up (and the Chinese *woman* is now my amazing wife).

I remember at one point, I was visiting a friend in Halifax and I raced back to Montreal, fifteen hours non-stop to be with her, imagining in my mind that I *was* Steve, speeding along single-lane highways doing my best to pass every car I could without smashing into oncoming traffic. But, it also put me in *his* mindset, the consummate race car driver. (Ok, ok, I did it in my Honda!)

I had some success with the early version of the script, getting it into the hands of the producer of "My Big Fat Greek Wedding" with the assistance of another producer from Vancouver who'd enthused over it. A couple of months were spent in giddy anticipation, waiting to hear back. Already, I was making imaginary down-payments on a new house. To no avail. The "My Big Fat Greek Wedding" producer liked the script, but he didn't see the commercial potential.

Deflated, the screenplay sat in my drawer for many years, forgotten.

However, I didn't realize that was just the *first act* of this story.

In 2018, along came Netflix, turning the movie industry upside down, offering to invest 500 million in Canadian productions. Suddenly, Hollywood wasn't so far away. There were pitch sessions in Montreal, where I live, and the Writer's Guild of Canada put us in contact. I submitted a good half-dozen synopsis of projects I'd been working on, and guess what? They wanted to hear more about Steve.

I went into the pitch session with a Taschen publication of Steve McQueen images and photos under my arm. The first question the *Director of Content Acquisition* at Netflix asked me was, "where's your producer?" I needed a producer? No one had told me. Still, they agreed to listen to my pitch. The head of content liked the idea and encouraged me to find a producer, making suggestions of who to contact. Of those producers, I had worked with one before, so that very evening I phoned him up. By the next day, we were off to the races (calling a producer and saying "I have Netflix interested" goes a long way, it seems).

I dusted off my old script and worked on it, now with many more years of experience under my belt.

My new producer liked the script, there was just one problem. Netflix was only going to cough up 5 million per Canadian production. *This* screenplay would cost much more than that, especially with its exotic locations. What to do?

Talking with my producer, I conceived of another project involving Steve, which centered more on his later career when he walked away from traditional Hollywood: a time when Steve refused parts in "Close Encounters of the Third Kind", "Apocalypse Now" and "Dirty Harry", to name just a few.

Everyone appeared to like this new approach, and so it was back to the drawing board (or blank page) for me. Another few months was spent writing, this time on a new treatment (i.e., a version of the script, but without the dialogues, so everyone can focus on the story. It's amazing in Hollywood how little time people spend *reading* scripts). I have to say, I had a great time with my new producer. He kept me on track with good notes, unlike some producers who don't know what they want and waste a lot of your time.

And here's where my personal story took another unexpected turn.

Working on this new concept, I was able to get in touch with Chad McQueen, Steve's son. We had many phone conversations, and he was extremely generous with his time and input, including teleconferencing with the former director of the Boys Republic reform school, where Steve had stayed as a youth. Chad gave me free reign on the story, an amazing thing in and of itself, but he was strict (and rightly so), making sure the details were correct and authentic. Often he'd say, "no, my dad wouldn't have done that," so it was back to reworking the material for me. One day, he pretty much floored me when he said, "yeah, I just had lunch with Steven (Spielberg), and the way my dad rejected Close Encounters didn't go down quite the way you wrote it, but don't worry about it, we'll talk more with Steven later..."

Needless to say, I was having a wonderful time writing, unmindful that reality was about to rear its ugly head once again.

As the treatment was being finished up, about a year after my first meeting with the execs from Netflix, they came back to us and said, sorry, we're not interested in *biopics* anymore. They didn't *even* want to read it.

In the end, I struggled, I had some emergency calls with my producer and finally they said, ok, we could at least send them the finished treatment we'd all worked so hard on. I don't think they ever bothered to read it. It was dead in the water. (Unfortunately, I can't reveal more about that particular project, as it's tied up in various non-disclosure agreements with Chad and others).

However, I wasn't ready to give up, not when I'd come so far. I still had my Young Steve McQueen script. Once again, I returned to it and did another pass on the screenplay—with my more recent insights.

Believe it or not, I was able to get it in the hands of Bryan Lourd, head of CAA talent agency and former husband of Carrie Fisher. As the agent for both George Clooney and Brad Pitt, he agreed to read it with the intention of presenting it to one or the other to produce. This was shortly after the release of Quentin Tarantino's "Once Upon a Time... in Hollywood", which includes a brief portrayal of Steve McQueen.

For a few weeks, I heard nothing. I followed up. And followed up again. Finally, Lourd's assistant got back to me: they had *shared* it. Yes, they liked the script enough to actually *share* it. (Whatever that means. Did George Clooney and Brad Pitt really read it?) For the next few days, I was on cloud nine, waiting for my cell phone to ring, to hear Brad or George's familiar voice (for some reason I more often imagined Brad Pitt's voice): "hey, let's do this."

But we all know... real life doesn't work like that (unless, you're Andy Weir). George and Brad kindly *passed*. Not much of a surprise mind you, since there aren't any good roles in it for them, maybe just some bit parts. Next, I got *this* script into the hands of the Coen Brothers' agent; I'm still waiting.

And then one day I figured, I'm done waiting. Now, the script has a chance to be in your hands, and you can decide its merits.

A few final comments about this screenplay. There are obviously lots of moments in Steve's life where no one can really know, now, what was said or what happened, and I've come across some contradictions as well, so I've had to fill in various blanks. No one I ever dealt with had much issue with this. The script is a *story*, after all, not a definitive historical record. One approach I took was a type of *flash forward*, where young Steve does something which recalls, or brings to mind, one of his later films, though obviously it couldn't actually have happened that way. Nevertheless, in exploring Steve's youth—his coming of age—I found there really was a mythic quality to it, something larger than life.

Yes, the film industry can be a fickle and frustrating business. One way or another, it's important for me to share Steve's story, both for the audience who already know his movies, but also for a new generation who will hopefully re-discover his work, as I did. There can be no doubt Steve McQueen left an indelible mark on cinema and beyond. His journey is a universal one, of overcoming incredible odds and struggling to find his place in a harsh world. This tale relates how the King of Cool was forged.

I hope you have as much pleasure reading it as I did writing, and in this way it can exist on the silver screen of our collective imagination.

D. R. Schoel
Montreal, June, 2020

ABOUT SCREENPLAY FORMATTING

For those new to film scripts, it should be noted that screenplays are written with the obvious intention of having them turned into movies—they are a road map for the film production team: director, actors, cinematographer, art directors, etc. As such, various conventions and terms are employed when writing a script. Film crews are generally aware of this terminology, helpful for organizing the logistics of their production.

Scene Headings begin by denoting the *location*: the entire film crew must decamp to this new local (which is why films tend to be filmed out-of-order, with *all* scenes at any given location recorded at the same time). The Scene Heading begins with either INT. *or* EXT: Interior or Exterior—an important differentiation since exterior scenes will, undoubtedly, have to contend with the weather, while interior scenes might occur in a studio or some other controlled location. This is followed by a brief description of the *place*, and the time of day (morning, sunset, night, etc).

Other terms you will come across are: *O.S.* for Off Screen, indicating someone is talking, but isn't seen on screen even though they're present and can be heard by the other characters (as well as the audience). *V.O.* is used for Voice Over to indicate a narrator or character's thoughts. When a character has a lengthier dialogue which is interrupted by descriptions, but no other character speaks in between, *CONT'D* is used to inform the actor it is to be spoken as an unbroken monologue.

Lastly, screenplays always use a Courier type font. This monospaced font was designed for typewriters where the letters are of equal proportion. While perhaps not the most aesthetically pleasing, it's become well established that a page of script written in Courier equals one minute of screen-time. In this way, a hundred and twenty page script would result in a two hour movie.

YOUNG STEVE MCQUEEN

written by
D.R. Schoel

EXT. AIRSTRIP -- MORNING

A dingy airstrip.

A subtitle reads: **Beech Grove, Indianapolis, 1930.**

A stunt pilot readies his biplane on the grassy
runway. This is "RED", with his back to the sun.
It's impossible to see his face.

Anxiously watching him is a twenty year-old blond
girl, JULLIAN, clutching a baby.

                    JULLIAN
          Red.
                    (no answer)
          Red?

He glances her way.

                    JULLIAN (CONT'D)
          What should I name the baby?

                    RED
          I owe my bookie, Steve, some
          cash. Name the kid Steve. Maybe
          that'll get the frickin' guy off
          my back.

Red gets into his plane and starts it.

                    JULLIAN
                    (yelling over the
                    engine)
          But when will you be back?!

Red doesn't answer.

His plane rolls down the runway and flies into the
rising sun.

Jullian, holding the baby tightly, watches him fly off. Baby Steve smiles, innocent, unaware of his mother's anguish.

EXT. THOMSON FARMSTEAD -- DAY

A large, rambling manor sits overlooking prime farmland.

A car approaches.

                    LILLIAN (Off Screen)
          I warned you! You never listen
          to me—

INT. THOMSON MANOR (HALLWAY) -- DAY

A camera P.O.V. wanders through the rustic farmhouse manor. It's like a labyrinth.

                    LILLIAN (O.S.)
          How many times did I say it?!
          It's your ways. Don't come
          running to me now. I can't help
          you!

INT. THOMSON MANOR (BEDROOM) -- DAY

Inside the bedroom, Jullian is hastily throwing clothes into a suitcase while her mother, LILLIAN, holds baby Steve in a blanket.

                    JULLIAN
          Ma — Put a sock in it!

She slams the suitcase shut and storms out of the room.

Lillian places baby Steve on the bed.

                    LILLIAN
          Lord, where did I go wrong?

INT. THOMSON MANOR (STAIRWELL) -- DAY

Lillian pursues her daughter down the stairs.

                    LILLIAN
          What do you expect me to do with
          that bastard of a child?

                    JULLIAN
          We live on a stinkin' hog farm,
          don't we? Raise him with the
          pigs for all I care!

INT/EXT. THOMSON MANOR (ENTRANCE) -- DAY

Jullian opens the front door, coming face to face
with an elderly man.

This is CLAUDE, kind looking with an old-fashioned
beard, covered with dust from working in the field.

He glances over his shoulder at the fancy car
idling in front of the house. A handsome man in the
driver seat politely waves.

Claude turns back to Jullian. His eyes speak
volumes.

                    JULLIAN
          I promise I'll come back for him,
          uncle. I just need some time.

She hurries past, into the waiting car.

INT. THOMSON MANOR (STAIRWELL) -- DAY

Claude wearily climbs the stairs to the bedroom.

INT. THOMSON MANOR (BEDROOM) -- DAY

Lying alone on the bed, baby Steve glances curiously at his new surroundings.

Removing his hat, Claude peers at the blond-haired, blue-eyed baby smiling sweetly.

> CLAUDE
> Now, what are we gonna do with
> you?

EXT. ST JOSEPH'S CATHOLIC CHURCH -- DAY

A rural church.

A subtitle reads: **seven years later.**

INT. ST JOSEPH'S CATHOLIC CHURCH -- MORNING

A blond, blue eyed boy —Steve— sits in a pew next to his grandmother, Lillian, her hands clutched tightly in prayer.

She mumbles, overwhelmed with religious sentiment, her eyes rolling back.

> PRIEST
> ...And he dreamed, and behold a
> ladder was set up on the earth,
> and the top of it reached to
> heaven; and angels of God were
> ascending and descending on it...

Steve stares at her red knuckles. He notices the
strange, fleeting looks cast by other churchgoers
at his grandmother.

>   PRIEST (CONT'D)
>   ...And the Lord stood above it,
>   and said, I am the God of
>   Abraham thy father, and the God
>   of Isaac: the land whereon thou
>   *liest*...

EXT. COUNTRY LANE -- MORNING

After the service, Steve walks up the country lane
with one hand in his grandmother's, the other
holding his shoes, treading barefoot.

>   CUT TO:

EXT. THOMSON FARMSTEAD -- DAY

Claude chops wood while Steve and his Irish Setter
watch.

>   CLAUDE
>   Gotta earn your keep, Stevie.

He hands him the ax. Steve swings with all his
might, barely denting the wood block.

>   CLAUDE (CONT'D)
>   Again. Show some muscle!

Steve swings.

The wood block splits in two and Steve smiles
triumphantly.

> CLAUDE (CONT'D)
> Alright. Finish the pile before
> lunch.

Claude ambles off. Steve turns and sees the massive heap of wood: it's impossible!

                                                    CUT TO:

EXT. STREAM -- DAY

Steve lazily lays on a riverbank with a fishing-string dangling in the water. The setter watches him.

                                                    CUT TO:

INT. THOMSON MANOR (LIVING ROOM) -- DAY

Claude has Steve over his knee with a hickory switch on his bare backside.

> CLAUDE
> I don't like dishing this out
> any more than you like takin' it
> in!

Wap!

Lillian wanders by carrying a basket full of laundry. She ignores Steve, who glances at her imploringly.

EXT. THOMSON MANOR -- DAY

Lillian hangs the laundry, while from inside the house — Harder.

Wap!

                    LILLIAN
                 (to herself)
        Cut from the same cloth as his
        good for nothin' mother.

                  CLAUDE (O.S.)
        If you'd only do your damn
        chores!

INT. THOMSON MANOR (LIVING ROOM) -- DAY

Steve struggles to keep the tears from flowing.

                                        CUT TO:

INT. THOMSON MANOR (ATTIC BEDROOM) -- EVENING

Steve sits on the windowsill of his attic bedroom.
Fiddle music wafts in.

                    STEVE
                 (to his dog)
        Ain't no big never mind...

Wiping his nose, he stares out the window at—

EXT. THOMSON FARMSTEAD (STEVE'S P.O.V.) -- EVENING

Lit by moonlight, the farmstead and valley spreads
into infinity. Magic.

Directly below, orange lamps dangle from fence
posts. People are dancing in the clearing between
the house and barn.

EXT. THOMSON FARMSTEAD -- CONTINUOUS

Lillian watches the revelers from the porch, scowling.

She doesn't notice Steve sneak by.

                                                CUT TO:

INT. BARN -- NIGHT

Claude is making love with a red-headed girl from behind, her skirt thrown over her back.

                    RED-HEAD
            Oh! Ride it Mr. Thomson! Ride
            it!

From a section of broken boards in the barn wall Steve crouches and stares.

                    CLAUDE
            I'm gonna ride you to town!

EXT. BARN -- NIGHT

Steve pushes a pig toward the opening. It's a stubborn beast.

                    STEVE
                (whispered)
            C'mon you!

                    RED-HEAD
            Oh! Oh!

Steve struggles while the pig *oinks* in protest.

Steve turns, and with a final shove from his rear-end, sends the pig scurrying through the opening.

INT. BARN -- NIGHT

The red-head sees the pig come rushing at her.

                    RED-HEAD
          Oh no!

She flees and Claude falls flat on a pile of hay.

EXT. BARN -- NIGHT

Ducking out of sight, Steve clutches his belly with
laughter.

INT. BARN -- NIGHT

Claude sighs in the hay.

                    CLAUDE
          Shit.

                                        CUT TO:

EXT. THOMSON LANE -- DAY

Steve sits proudly next to his uncle who's driving
an open-roofed car up a dirt lane.

Others are on horseback or on foot for a Saturday
morning stroll.

                    CLAUDE
          See them poles?

Steve glances at the telephone polls along the road,
where workers are busily erecting a new line.

                    CLAUDE (CONT'D)
          That line runs straight on up to
          our livin' room. The only
          private line in Slater!

Steve cranes his neck to proudly trace the wire
through the air as they drive past.

Claude, meanwhile, spots the red-head walking arm-
in-arm with another man.

                    CLAUDE (CONT'D)
          The she-devil! She's with my
          brother, dammit!

He suddenly veers and pulls a revolver from his
jacket.

The red-head and Claude's brother turn.

                    RED-HEAD
          Mr. Thomson?

                    BROTHER
          Claude—?

                    CLAUDE
          Get your hands off her!

He hops out of the car and the revolver
accidentally goes off *CRACK*!

His brother tumbles to the ground, holding his arm.

                    CLAUDE (CONT'D)
          Holy shit! I killed him!

Steve leans over the windshield, gawking.

                                        CUT TO:

INT. THOMSON MANOR (LIVING ROOM) -- DAY

Lillian is knitting when the phone rings.

She looks at it uncertainly, unused to the device.

She picks up the receiver.

                    LILLIAN
          Hello?

She listens.

                    LILLIAN (CONT'D)
          What do you mean you're going to
          be late?

                                        CUT TO:

INT. MOVIE PALACE -- DAY

A B-Western is playing.

Steve, replete with cowboy hat, sits next to his
uncle... next to the red-head... sandwiched between
Claude's brother, his arm in a sling. Steve's
engrossed in the movie, transported.

                                        CUT TO:

EXT. THOMSON FARMSTEAD (PIG PENS) -- MORNING

Glorious sunshine. A herd of hogs stream into pig
pens.

Steve runs wildly among the pigs with his dog,
herding the animals into pens.

EXT. THOMSON FARMSTEAD -- MOMENTS LATER

Shutting the gate on the hogs, Steve climbs the
fence post, proudly surveying his lands. Then—

>   LILLIAN (O.S.)
>   Who among you has not sinned?!
>   Let him cast the first stone!

It's Steve's grandmother, naked, holding a crucifix
over her head, bible in hand.

>   LILLIAN (CONT'D)
>   God's wrath will descend on ye
>   as it did in Sodom—

Some workers in the field shake their heads. Steve
turns and just as quickly glances down, shame-faced.

>   WORKER
>   It's that crazy Thomson woman.

>   CLAUDE
>   Lillian!

Claude comes hurrying from the manor, throwing a
blanket around his sister.

>   CLAUDE (CONT'D)
>   Get hold of yourself!

>   LILLIAN
>   Claude?

>   CLAUDE
>   What in god's name possessed
>   you?

>   LILLIAN
>   He speaks through me. I'm
>   tellin' you—

                    CLAUDE
        Well he ain't got nothing more
        to say! Let's go.

He leads her up the lane when he spots Steve rooted
by the fence. Uncle Claude reads the uncertainty in
Steve's face.

                    CLAUDE (CONT'D)
        C'mon. You too. We're going home.

Head bowed, he follows Claude and his grandmother
up the lane.

                                        FADE OUT:

EXT. THOMSON FARMSTEAD (TRAIN CAR) -- EVENING

In the rosy hews of sunset, Steve treks through the
long grass with his dog. Across the field is an
abandoned train car.

He stops in front of the rusting vehicle. The
setter whines.

                    STEVE
        Quiet, Jim.

Steve mounts a wooden step and gently pushes open
the door.

INT. TRAIN CAR -- EVENING

The train car has been converted into a rustic home.

The walls are covered with Civil War era
paraphernalia, lit by musty candles.

Steve's grandmother sits by a table, knitting. She glances up, then resumes her knitting.

>   LILLIAN
>   This farm's been ours for three
>   generations—

Steve, arms at his sides, listens obediently.

>   LILLIAN (CONT'D)
>   The Thomsons came to Saline from
>   Scotland and we've fought every
>   war since the Revolution. Your
>   great great-grand-daddy, Pike
>   Montgomery Thomson, was captured
>   by the Yankees and was to stand
>   before the firin' squad, but the
>   Captain who was holdin' him
>   suddenly took with a bout of
>   conscience. Do you know what
>   this Yankee's name was?

Steve doesn't answer.

>   LILLIAN (CONT'D)
>   Don't stand there like a deaf-
>   mute. I know you can hear me. Do
>   you know what his name was?

>   STEVE
>   No, ma'am.

>   LILLIAN
>   McQueen. Just like your
>   disappearin' daddy. Ain't that a
>   coincidence? It took two
>   McQueen's to bring you into this
>   rotten world.

Steve opens his hand, placing two chicken eggs in front of her.

                    LILLIAN (CONT'D)
          What's this?

She picks them up.

                    LILLIAN (CONT'D)
          Did you bring these for me?

Steve nods shyly.

                    LILLIAN (CONT'D)
          What'd I tell you about
          stealin'?!

She squeezes her hand, crushing the eggs. Yolk
drips on the floor.

                    LILLIAN (CONT'D)
          They've locked me up!

Steve rushes for the door.

EXT. THOMSON FARMSTEAD (TRAIN CAR) -- NIGHT

He runs from the train car.

                    LILLIAN (O.S.)
          You'll never escape from here!

                                        DISSOLVE TO:

EXT. THOMSON FARMSTEAD -- MORNING

The sun is golden over the Thomson fields.

INT. BARN -- MORNING

Steve is busy milking a cow.

                    CLAUDE (O.S.)
          Stevie?

Steve looks up. Claude is silhouetted in the
entrance, gripping a hunting rifle. He kneels
next to the boy.

                    CLAUDE (CONT'D)
          Here.

He hands the rifle to Steve.

                    CLAUDE (CONT'D)
          You can use it for game.
          There're quail by the river.

Steve holds the rifle in his tiny hands, turning it
over in religious-like awe. Claude holds up a
single bullet.

                    CLAUDE (CONT'D)
          Only one.

He puts it in Steve's hand.

                    CLAUDE (CONT'D)
          Use it well.

                    STEVE
          But—

                    CLAUDE
          Don't talk back to your elders.

                                        CUT TO:

EXT. STREAM -- DAY

Steve walks along the stream, lugging the hunting
rifle.

He's fixated on the single bullet in his hand.

He slides it into the rifle's firing chamber.

EXT. THOMSON FARMSTEAD (PIG PENS) -- DAY

Uncle Claude is feeding his pigs, sweating in the hot sun.

A gunshot rings out.

He rushes to the gate, searching the horizon.

Lillian steps onto the porch of her train car, squinting.

With his hand over his eyes, Claude spots Steve in the distance, strolling through the fields — returning to the farm. Smiling proudly, Steve holds up two pigeons.

Lillian glowers while Uncle Claude beams with disbelief.

                              SLOW FADE OUT:

INT. THOMSON MANOR (KITCHEN) -- MORNING

Claude, his hair a little grayer, is busy cooking by the stove.

Through the kitchen window, Claude notices a car stop by the house. He examines it for a long moment, furrowing his brow.

                    CLAUDE
          Stevie? You'd better come on
          down.

No answer. Claude repeats himself, louder.

                    CLAUDE (CONT'D)
          Stevie! You hear me?!

Glancing at the ceiling (at the attic above),
Claude hears Steve roll blindly out of bed and
THUMP onto the floor.

                    STEVE (O.S.)
          Ow!

This is followed by more clambering about. Jim, the
old setter, eyes the ceiling and whines.

At last, Steve comes bounding down. He's in his
teens, wiry, blond and blue-eyed. He catches
Claude's eye.

                    STEVE (CONT'D)
          Uncle?

Claude nods toward the window.

EXT. THOMSON MANOR -- CONTINUOUS

A woman steps out of the car. It's Jullian, Steve's
mother.

She looks around as if the farm was a distant
memory.

                                        CUT TO:

INT. BERRI'S CAR -- DAY

Steve sits in the back of the car clutching a
suitcase, while his mother sits in the front
passenger seat. A heavy-set man drives, BERRI.

The car pulls away from the farm, where Claude
stands on the porch with Jim.

EXT. THOMSON FARMSTEAD (TRAIN CAR) -- DAY

Berri's car kicks up a cloud of dust as it drives
past the train car. From a shuttered window,
Lillian scowls.

EXT. THOMSON MANOR -- DAY

Claude, clouded with uncertainty, watches the car
disappear around a bend.

                    CLAUDE
                 (resigned)
          C'mon, Jim.

They go inside.

INT. BERRI'S CAR -- DAY

Jullian watches Steve from the rear-view-mirror.
He's anxious, unsure.

She turns to him, smiling, trying to put on a brave
face.

But she's like an uneasy bird.

                    JULLIAN
          This's Berri.

                    STEVE
          Sir.

                    BERRI
          Hi, Steve.

                    JULLIAN
          He's my husband.

Steve doesn't know what to say. He glances out the
window.

                    JULLIAN (CONT'D)
          That pig farm's no place for a
          beautiful boy like you. Berri
          an' me are all set up in the
          city now. Won't that be more
          fun?

Steve, sullen, doesn't answer.

                    JULLIAN (CONT'D)
          I — I know I've been away. But
          I'll make it up to you in spades.

Her expression becomes serious.

EXT. HIGHWAY -- DAY

The car passes beneath an L.A. street sign.

                              DISSOLVE TO:

EXT. BERRI'S APARTMENT -- EVENING

Berri's car is parked in front of an apartment
building on a half-paved road of cheap motels.

INT. BERRI'S APARTMENT (STEVE'S ROOM) -- EVENING

Steve unpacks his few belongings into the only
dresser.

There's a small bed, but otherwise the room is bare.

Jullian sticks her head in.

                    JULLIAN
          So, how'd ya like it?

                    STEVE
          S'all right.

                    JULLIAN
          It's a start.
               (glancing around the
               room)
          You could hang a picture of
          Jimmy Cagney right here—
               (framing her hands)
          You like him, don't you? Berri,
          you know, works in the motion
          picture business.

                    STEVE
          Uh-huh.

                    JULLIAN
          Is that all you have to say?

                    STEVE
          What do you want me to say?

                    JULLIAN
          You c'n call me... mom, for
          starters.

Steve stares at her.

                        JULLIAN (CONT'D)
          Alright. I know. It ain't been
          easy for me either.
                    (beat)
          Berri's great. You two'll get
          along famously, I know it.

                                        CUT TO:

EXT. BERRI'S APARTMENT -- NIGHT

Steve sits on the fire-escape next to his open
window.

He stares at the bleak, grimy neighborhood. A long
way from the farm.

                                        CUT TO:

INT. STUDIO -- DAY

Black.

One by one, the overhead lights turn on.

Steve follows Berri to the back of the empty studio
where movie lights and equipment are stored.
TEAMSTERS are sorting lamp-heads and cabling.

                        TEAMSTER
          Hey, kid. Got your union card?

                        STEVE
          Sir?

                        BERRI
          It's my old lady's boy. Gonna
          put him to work.

                    TEAMSTER
          Welcome to Hollywood.

                                                CUT TO:

INT. STUDIO -- MOMENTS LATER

The teamster places a dozen rolled up lengths of
cable over Steve's shoulders, like a mountain
climber. He staggers under the weight.

                                                CUT TO:

INT. STUDIO -- MOMENTS LATER

Steve precariously climbs a steep ladder to an
overhead catwalk.

On all fours, he crawls along the catwalk,
unslinging the electric cables. Finished, he
glances down at the studio floor:

                    TEAMSTER
                   (to Berri)
          ...Yeah, think I knew a Bill
          McQueen. Over in Silver Lake.
          Rumored he flew with the Flying
          Tigers, but people'll say
          anything to get work in this
          town.

Steve ponders.

                                                CUT TO:

INT. STUDIO -- MOMENTS LATER

Berri and the teamster lift a heavy light from the
storage rack.

> BERRI
> ...figure I can run 'em like my
> own private Stalag. Warm pussy
> at night and her kid can earn
> some extra bucks.

> TEAMSTER
> Sounds like got yourself one
> helluva of a P.O.W. camp.

> BERRI
> Speakin' of which, where is that
> stick in the mud?
>> (angry shout)
> Steve?!

They look up at the catwalk, but there's no sign of
Steve.

>> CUT TO:

EXT. STUDIO -- DAY

Steve finds a phone booth near the street.

INT. PHONE BOOTH -- DAY

He tears out a page from the phone book.

>> CUT TO:

EXT. L.A. STREET -- DAY

Steve rides his bike, glancing at the torn page.

He stops in front of a hardware store.

INT. HARDWARE STORE -- DAY

The shopkeeper glances at the torn paper in Steve's hand.

              SHOPKEEPER
     'Bout 3 blocks east. Take a
     right.

              STEVE
     Much obliged.

Steve heads to the door.

              SHOPKEEPER
     Hey! Haven't I seen you around?
     Or maybe your daddy's been in?

Hopeful—

              STEVE
     Could be.

                        CUT TO:

EXT. RUNDOWN APARTMENT BUILDING -- DAY

Steve parks in front of a rundown apartment building pleading to be demolished.

INT. RUNDOWN APARTMENT BUILDING -- DAY

Inside, Steve stares at the apartment door bearing
the number in the phone book. Finally, he knocks.

There's no answer.

He tries the handle.

INT. RED'S APARTMENT -- DAY

The door opens.

Steve steps into the apartment.

He explores the empty, dust-filled rooms with
peeling strips of paint for any sign of his father.
Voices from the past, like ghosts, emanate from the
walls.

                    RED (O.S.)
                 (distant)
        I owe my bookie, Steve, some
        cash. Name the kid Steve...

                    JULLIAN (O.S.)
                 (distant)
        But when will you be back...?

Sunlight through the window catches something on
the floor.

Steve approaches... and discovers a lighter with a
biplane and the word "Red" engraved on it. He looks
it over, before sticking it in his jeans.

INT. RUNDOWN APARTMENT BUILDING -- DAY

Disappointed, Steve exits the apartment. On the
landing, he spots a scruffy, lanky teen lounging in
the stairwell. Steve rushes past with the ominous
feeling he's being watched.

He glances over his shoulder.

                    LANKY KID
          What're you starin' at?

Steve hurries down the stairs.

As he passes a broken window, he slips a shard of
glass, knife-like, into the palm of his hand,
hiding it in his sleeve.

Suddenly, someone leaps out and presses him against
the wall, their hand around his throat.

                    BILLY
          Who're you looking for?

It's a kid about the same size as Steve, with a
pock-marked face and jet black hair.

                    STEVE
          Sorry. Wrong address.

                    BILLY
          You lookin' funny at my pal over
          there?

                    STEVE
          Just mindin' my own.

Steve grips the glass-shard in his hand; five
others are coming up the stairwell.

                    BILLY
          This here's condemned land, or
          didn't they teach you to read
          back on the farm? Gonna hafta
          fine you for trespassing.

Steve's fear diminishes as he formulates a plan.

                    STEVE
          Make no never mind to me.

Billy lets go and Steve brushes past, toward the
door.

                    BILLY
          Just where the fuck you going?

                    STEVE
          I got nothin' on me.

He goes out. Billy looks at the others and shrugs.

EXT. RUNDOWN APARTMENT BUILDING -- DAY

Steve tosses the shard of glass aside.

The others quickly follow with Steve in the lead.

EXT. HARDWARE STORE -- DAY

Steve approaches the hardware store. As he opens
the door, Billy grabs him by the arm.

                    BILLY
No tricks, man. We'll brain you
so good, you won't know up from
down.

                    STEVE
Alright. You just wait here.

He goes in.

INT. HARDWARE STORE -- DAY

Casually, Steve browses the racks, glancing at the
shopkeeper by the counter. Next, he scans the
window, where Billy and the gang kids are keeping
an eye on him.

EXT. HARDWARE STORE -- DAY

                    BILLY
          What's he up to?

INT. HARDWARE STORE -- DAY

Steve selects a wrench and approaches the
shopkeeper.

                    STEVE
          My father bought this a couple
          of weeks ago. He's been late
          getting to the plumbing. But
          it's the wrong size.

                    SHOPKEEPER
You want to exchange it?

                    STEVE
          That's alright. The super took
          care of it.

Steve pushes the wrench across the counter.

                    SHOPKEEPER
          Ok...

The shopkeeper rings up the cash-register.

EXT. HARDWARE STORE -- DAY

Steve exits the hardware store where the gang kids
are waiting. He counts out the money, handing half
to Billy.

                    STEVE
          Here's your share, for the
          inspiration.

Billy takes the money.

                    BILLY
          You're one clever hick.

He extends his hand. They shake.

                    STEVE
          Buddy Berri...
                    (correcting himself)
          Steve.

INT. BERRI'S APARTMENT (KITCHEN) -- NIGHT

The fridge opens and Steve, in high spirits, grabs
a soda bottle, popping off the cap.

                    BERRI (O.S.)
          So, where'd you disappear to?

Berri appears in the doorway, nursing a beer.

                    STEVE
          Where's Jullian?

                    BERRI
          You mean, your ma?

He sticks a thumb over his shoulder.

INT. BERRI'S APARTMENT (LIVING ROOM) -- NIGHT

Jullian's passed out on the sofa, dangling a beer
bottle. A bruise is visible on her shoulder.

                    STEVE
          Mom—?

He moves the beer bottle aside before it spills.
She stirs.

                    JULLIAN
          Steve?

                    STEVE
          What'd you do to her?

                    BERRI
        You didn't answer me. You think
        you're some city slicker all of
        a sudden? Where were you?

                    STEVE
        What makes you think I have to
        listen to you? You're not my
        father—

Without warning, Berri wallops Steve across the
face. He falls to the floor.

                    BERRI
        That's why you gotta listen to
        me! I'm all you've got, so you
        better goddamn well learn to
        follow the rules!

Jullian props herself up, her arms reaching for
Berri in supplication.

                    JULLIAN
        Berri! Please!

Berri smacks Jullian—

                    BERRI
        Fuck you and your candy ass kid!
        You're stinkin' drunk, you dirty
        whore!

She mollifies him, moving his hand to her breast.

                    JULLIAN
        Berri...

Berri pushes her toward the bedroom.

Steve wipes blood from his nose, absorbing his new family situation.

> BERRI (O.S.)
> Cheap sluts like you are a dime
> a dozen round here.

FADE OUT:

EXT. MOVIE PALACE -- DAY

Crowds pass an old-time movie palace.

INT. MOVIE PALACE -- DAY

Steve sits next to his mother, watching a movie. She's well dressed, having taken Steve for a treat.

Steve's engrossed in the film. Jullian watches him in the flickering light. She leans near and whispers.

> JULLIAN
> It was my fault.
> (thinking)
> When I get to drinkin'...
> Berri's a good man and
> discipline ain't a bad thing.

From the shadows, Steve watches her.

> STEVE
> What was my father like?

> JULLIAN
> Berri's your father now.

CUT TO:

EXT. ASYLUM -- DAY

Berri leans against his car, parked outside Fulton
State Hospital, smoking a cigarette.

INT. ASYLUM (HALLWAY) -- DAY

Jullian's high heels click along the floor of the
sanitarium.

Steve is by her side.

INT. ASYLUM (PATIENT'S ROOM) -- DAY

Lillian sits facing the window. A dinner tray has
been thrown on the floor, by her feet.

She appears to be in a semi-catatonic state.

                    JULLIAN
          Oh, ma... Look what you've done.

Lillian's eyes flicker. No acknowledgement.

Steve idles by the door while his mother cleans up
the tray.

                    JULLIAN (CONT'D)
          Have they been treating you
          well?

Jullian spots a brush on the table and
instinctively picks it up.

                    JULLIAN (CONT'D)
          That's all you've got to wear? I
          can pick you up something.

She reaches to brush the older woman's hair — when
Lillian raises a hand. She sees Steve's reflection
in the window.

                    LILLIAN
          Who's the idiot deaf-mute? Is
          that Steve?

Steve glares at his grandmother. He turns and
storms out.

                    JULLIAN
          Ma — how dare you talk to him—?

She steps toward Lillian, who grabs her eating
knife, aiming it at her daughter.

                    LILLIAN
          You're the devil's spawn!

EXT. ASYLUM -- DAY

Steve shakily exits.

Noticing Berri's leering, watchful gaze, Steve
glares defiantly at him and sets off down the
street. Berri snickers.

INT. ASYLUM (PATIENT'S ROOM) -- DAY

Inside, Jullian stares coldly at her mother.

                    JULLIAN
         They're gonna lock you up for
         good this time, ma! Or, don't
         you remember! It ain't the first
         time you've pointed a knife at
         me!

                    LILLIAN
         I should'a killed you when I had
         the chance.

                    JULLIAN
         And you should'a killed yourself
         while you were at it, but you
         couldn't even do that properly!

                    LILLIAN
         Shut up! Shut up!

She glances at the thin, long-since healed scars on
her wrist.

                    JULLIAN
         Why do you think I go out
         boozing and fucking anything
         that moves?

The knife shakes in Lillian's hand.

                    JULLIAN (CONT'D)
         You might as well get it over
         with! Your daughter's a whore
         and her life ain't worth shit,
         and you know I left 'cause I
         couldn't bear the thought I'd do
         the same to Steve! It was
         because of you! It was all
         because of you and your voices
         and I hope you rot forever! God
         doesn't speak to you! He
         doesn't give a damn about you!

Lillian drops the knife, raising her hands to her face.

There isn't a drop of compassion in Jullian's frigid glare.

EXT. ASYLUM -- DAY

Jullian angrily stomps out of the asylum.

                    JULLIAN
          Where's Steve?!

EXT. ALLEY -- DAY

Steve, stewing, marches down an alley, angrily kicking at a cat. *Meow!*

He comes out into the street—

EXT. STREET -- DAY

—Pushing through a throng of people, where he nearly gets bowled over by an elephant! It blasts its trunk at him. Steve stumbles backwards, onto his ass.

A hand helps him up.

                    CARNIE
          Y'alright, kid?

Steve brushes himself off, taking in the sight of the ten penny circus passing through.

                    CARNIE (CONT'D)
        Oh, I can spot talent a mile
        away, and you have it kid. Yes,
        son, you can see the world, make
        great money selling pencils.
        Whadaya say?

                                    CUT TO:

EXT. ASYLUM -- DAY

Jullian's frantically looking for Steve.

                    JULLIAN
        What do you mean, he just
        marched off? You didn't try to
        stop him?

                    BERRI
        Far as I'm concerned, he's old
        enough to look after his' self.

                    JULLIAN
        Fuck you. He's just a kid.

Regardless, she gets in the car, scowling. Berri
starts the engine.

                                    CUT TO:

EXT. CIRCUS -- DAY

Steve watches while a circus big-top is put up.

                                DISSOLVE TO:

EXT. CIRCUS -- LATER

Crowds mill past. Steve's at a table among a row of
booths and tents: the circus sideshow.

> STEVE
> Pen and pencil sets, only a buck
> twenty five—

> PASSERBY
> Screw you.

> STEVE
> (grumbling)
> Bunch of freaks.

The circus worker who first enticed Steve ambles up
from behind.

> CARNIE
> You fit right in here.

Steve ignores him.

> CARNIE (CONT'D)
> Aren't those fer fifty cents?

Steve reaches into his cash box.

> STEVE
> Ok, here's thirty percent of my
> take, now lay off.

> CARNIE
> Better make it fifty.

Steve counts out some more cash. The carnie laughs
hoarsely and meanders off. Steve closes up his cash
box, dispirited.

FADE OUT:

EXT. CIRCUS (ANOTHER LOCATION) -- NIGHT

In the dim of night, lions snort in their cages and elephants sleep standing up.

Steve's asleep under the stars on a makeshift mattress amongst junk, boxes, crates, etc. He flinches, groaning.

Steve cocks open an eye. He sees a drunk shamble past, drinking out of a whiskey bottle. Finishing his last drop, the man dashes his bottle — *crash!*

No one pays him the least attention. The drunk stumbles... then collapses. Silence reigns. Steve stares at the slumped form.

He glances about. All's quiet. Steve throws off his covers.

He sneaks over. Carefully, he lays a hand on the drunk's back. He's breathing.

Like a snake, Steve rummages through the man's pockets, pulling out a handful of change.

                                        CUT TO:

EXT. TRAIN -- NIGHT

A train clatters past. Steve throws his bag in an open boxcar, clambering in after it.

                                        CUT TO:

INT / EXT. TRAIN CAR -- NIGHT

Huddled with his arms around his knees, Steve sits
by the open door, staring outside. Rolling hills
slide by under the glittering stars.

Steve's breath is visible in the cold air. The
rattle of the train gently rocks him to sleep.

                                        CUT TO:

INT. TRAIN CAR -- NIGHT

The train has stopped. Steve's snoring.

Voices. A dog barks.

Steve opens his eyes, catching sight of a
flashlight beam nearby. Like a cat, he slides into
the darkest corner of the train car. The flashlight
passes him by.

                    VOICE (O.S.)
            There he is—

Suddenly, voices. An argument. Scuffling. Steve
stares into the darkness, terrified.

                    VOICE (O.S.) (CONT'D)
            Sick 'em boy.

The dog growls and barks, giving chase after
someone. The sounds fade. Steve edges to the open
door and carefully peeks out.

Nothing. The train starts up again.

                                        CUT TO:

EXT. TRAIN -- MORNING

The train chatters through a steep mountain pass,
bathed in the rosy hews of dawn.

INT / EXT. TRAIN CAR -- MORNING

Steve takes in the breathtaking view.

                                        CUT TO:

EXT. BERRI'S APARTMENT -- DAY

Bag thrown over his shoulder, Steve stares at the
building where Berri and his mother live. Back home.

INT. BERRI'S APARTMENT (KITCHEN) -- DAY

Steve slinks into the apartment.

Berri's having a beer with some stew in the kitchen.
He spots Steve.

                    BERRI
          'Bout time you came crawlin'
          back.

Steve glares at him.

                                        CUT TO:

EXT. EMPTY LOT -- DAY

Steve throws a punch: It's a rumble between two
street gangs!

The guy opposite Steve falls like a rock.

Steve pommels him relentlessly.

EXT. BIRD'S EYE VIEW OF EMPTY LOT -- CONTINUOUS

In the center of the action, Steve beats his prone
opponent with his fists, full of pent up anger. His
gang members chase off the other fleeing kids.

EXT. EMPTY LOT -- CONTINUOUS

Steve keeps on punching.

                                            CUT TO:

EXT. L.A. STREET -- MORNING

A hubcap tumbles to the pavement. Steve grabs his
crowbar and scurries around the car to the next
wheel, while Billy (the gang member he met while
searching for his father) keeps lookout.

                     BILLY
            Shake a leg, Steve—

Out of the corner of his eye, Steve spots two guys
exit a bar across the street, headed in their
direction. One of them is jangling car keys.

                     STEVE
            Shit.

He scoops up the hubcaps, breaking into a run.

                     BILLY
            Steve? Where'd you—?

                     CAR OWNER
            Hey! You!

The owner of the car comes rushing up.

Steve pauses at the street corner, glancing back. The owner of the car grabs Billy while his friend punches him. Steve hesitates. Should he help?

He turns and hightails it, running in the opposite direction when a police cruiser pulls up, lights flashing *WOOP WOOP*.

Steve's caught red handed, dangling the hubcaps at his side.

                                        CUT TO:

INT. POLICE CRUISER -- DAY

Steve nervously watches while the officer parks by Berri's apartment.

EXT. BERRI'S APARTMENT -- DAY

With a gentle push, the officer propels Steve toward the door.

INT. BERRI'S APARTMENT (LANDING) -- DAY

The door opens and Berri glances at Steve and the police officer.

                    COP
          Afternoon, sir. Your boy here—

                    BERRI
          My boy? He's not my—

                    COP
          —Was caught lifting hubcaps.
          We'll leave it at a warning this
          time, seeing he's a minor, but
          next time there'll be charges.
          You aught to keep a better eye
          on him.

The officer tips his hat and withdraws.

                                        CUT TO:

EXT. BERRI'S APARTMENT -- DAY

The police cruiser drives away.

INT. BERRI'S APARTMENT (LANDING) -- DAY

Berri blocks the entrance to the apartment.

                    STEVE
          Can I come in?

Berri doesn't budge.

Steve makes an about face, figuring Berri needs
time to cool off.

Without warning, Berri's rage boils over and he
punches Steve in the back.

                    BERRI
          You little shit! Bringing the
          cops to my door!

He shoves Steve down the stairs, sending him
flying!

Steve lies crumpled on the landing, motionless.

                    BERRI (CONT'D)
          Steve?! Stop playing around.

Finally, Steve gets to his feet, bleeding from the
mouth.

He points an accusing finger.

                    STEVE
          Lay your hands on me again and
          I'll kill you!

Berri steps back in fear.

                                        CUT TO:

EXT. COURTHOUSE -- DAY

Berri's car is parked in front of a local
courthouse.

INT. COURTROOM -- DAY

Jullian, disconsolate, sits next to a legal advisor,
while Berri —in his best suit— speaks to the judge.

                    BERRI
          —We've tried everything your
          honor, but he's incorrigible.

                    JUDGE
             (absently rifling
             through a file)
          Your boy, Terrence Steven
          McQueen, has been pulled in 3
          times for lifting hubcaps, twice
          for misdemeanors, there've been
          2 complaints of assault, one of
          which has been dropped while the
          other's pending...

He looks over his glasses at Jullian.

                    JUDGE (CONT'D)
          You consider sending him to
          reformatory school the only
          recourse?

                    BERRI
          That's correct, your honor.

Berri glances at Jullian. She reluctantly nods
consent.

                    JUDGE
          Then I see no reason to disagree
          with you.

The judge scribbles on a form and passes it to the
clerk, who puts it on the table for Jullian to sign.

                    JUDGE (CONT'D)
          Hopefully, the state can turn
          young Mr. McQueen into a fine,
          upstanding young man before it's
          too late. Next case.

Jullian stares at the paper.

                    BERRI
                 (whispering)
          It's for the best.

Doubtful, she signs.

                                        CUT TO:

EXT. JUNIOR BOYS REPUBLIC (COURTYARD) -- DAY

Steve stands in a courtyard among a row of boys.

The headmaster, FRANK GRAVES, gives the boys the
lowdown, standing on the porch of a squat building.

                    FRANK GRAVES
          Each of you must fulfill a daily
          work requirement. Two hours a
          day tending crops and livestock,
          in the laundry, kitchen, offices
          or auto maintenance. Work habits
          are of paramount importance.
          Getting to a job on time, taking
          direction from a supervisor...

Some of the boys fidget, while the headmaster
continues:

                    FRANK GRAVES (CONT'D)
          You will be self-governed. You
          will live in teams, and each
          team will elect two council
          members who, in turn, elect the
          mayor of our republic. There
          will be weekly town hall
          meetings, open to all. This
          Boys Republic has no walls, no
          guards, no cells. Our system is
          based on trust. Discipline will
          be swift.

                    STEVE
               (under his breath)
          What a load of garbage.

Another boy, a veteran of the Boys Republic, hands
Steve a clothing tag.

                    BOY
          You're 3-1-8-8.

Steve turns the tag over in his hand, taking note
of his new "identity number".

EXT. JUNIOR BOYS REPUBLIC (COURTYARD) -- NIGHT

Night falls over the barren grounds: half-a-dozen
sparse cabins.

INT. JUNIOR BOYS REPUBLIC (CABIN) -- NIGHT

Steve lies in a bunk bed staring at the ceiling.
Other boys snore.

He pulls the Zippo lighter with the word "Red"
engraved on it from under his pillow, turning it
over thoughtfully in the glinting moonlight.

                              DISSOLVE TO:

EXT. JUNIOR BOYS REPUBLIC (CABIN) -- DAY

The kids march out of their cabin, one by one,
shaking their linen, while others are busy sweeping
or cleaning the windows.

Lazily, Steve tosses a baseball, bouncing it off
the cabin's wall... contemplating how to make his
"great escape".

                    KID
          Hey — McQueer! You a sucker for
          punishment?

Steve glowers at him.

> STEVE
> It make no never-mind to me.

Overseeing another cabin's cleanup, the headmaster,
Frank Graves, spots Steve goofing off.

> CUT TO:

EXT. FARM -- DAY

Steve jogs along rolling farmland, hopping over a
fence.

> CUT TO:

INT. BARN -- DAY

Steve lies curled in a pile of hay, snoozing.

A horse nuzzles his hair. Sleepily, Steve waves it
away with his hand.

EXT. BARN -- DAY

A police cruiser is stopped in front of the barn.

> CUT TO:

INT. JUNIOR BOYS REPUBLIC (CLASSROOM) -- DAY

Steve stands with his hands behind his back in
front of three boys: his judges.

The rest of Steve's team-mates are lined up behind
him. They glare at his back.

                    BOYS MAYOR
          For attempting to run away from
          the Republic, we sentence you to
          five days urinal duty—

                      STEVE
                    (mouthing)
          Kiss my balls.

                    BOYS MAYOR
          And your entire team will lose
          its privileges for a week.

                      KID
          What? We didn't do nothing!

                    BOYS MAYOR
          Those are the rules.

Steve's team-mates grumble.

                                        CUT TO:

INT. URINAL -- DAY

Steve is on his hands and knees, scrubbing a toilet.

                                        CUT TO:

INT. JUNIOR BOYS REPUBLIC (MACHINE SHOP) -- DAY

In the machine shop, Steve's focused on his
solitary work.

He's good with tools.

But he doesn't notice when his team-mates sneak up
behind him.

Three boys grab him.

52

                         STEVE
               Hey! Get off me!

They cover his mouth.

                         KID
               Over here! Put him here!

The boys slam Steve behind a machine, hidden from
view.

                         KID (CONT'D)
               You think you're better than the
               rest of us?

One of the boys punches Steve in the stomach.

                         STEVE
               Ah!

The noise of the machine shop drowns him out; the
supervisor is oblivious. The kids glower at Steve,
bloody vengeance in their eyes.

The lead kid picks up a pipe, slamming Steve flat
on the stomach.

                         KID
               That's so you won't forget.

He drops the pipe and goes out. Steve grimaces,
writhing on the floor.

                         STEVE
               Ahg—!

The other boys silently troop out, leaving Steve
alone and in pain.

                                        CUT TO:

EXT. JUNIOR BOYS REPUBLIC (COURTYARD) -- MORNING

Doing his rounds, Frank Graves walks past the schoolhouse.

> MISS GRAVES (O.S.)
> Every president since Calvin
> Coolidge has hung a Della Robbia
> Christmas wreath in the White
> House, made right here at the
> Boys Republic—

INT. JUNIOR BOYS REPUBLIC (CLASSROOM) -- DAY

The boys stand behind their desks, watching Miss Graves. A row of boxes have been laid in front of her. She holds up a Christmas Wreath.

> MISS GRAVES
> Our founder, Margaret Fowler, in
> 1923, patterned this wreath off
> of 15th century ceramic wreaths
> made by the Della Robbia family
> in Florence, Italy.

Steve's expression is zombie-like.

> MISS GRAVES (CONT'D)
> It represents California's
> natural beauty and abundance.
> They are sold in every state in
> the union and shipped overseas.
> The Della Robbia wreath is the
> life-blood of the Boys Republic.

Steve groans.

> MISS GRAVES (CONT'D)
> And as you know, our motto is—?

All the boys except Steve:

                    BOYS
                (in unison)
        Nothing Without Labor!

                  MISS GRAVES
        Very good. Now if you come
        closer—
                (indicating the
                boxes)
        You'll see the wreaths are made
        from pinecones, cotton burs,
        eucalyptus, teasel, lemon and
        apples...

                              DISSOLVE TO:

INT. JUNIOR BOYS REPUBLIC (CLASSROOM) -- LATER

The boys are hard at work making wreaths. Steve
glances about, then swiftly grabs something from
his team-mate's box of materials.

                    KID
        Did you just steal one of my
        pinecones?

                    STEVE
                (infantile
                repetition)
        You just steal one of my
        pinecones?

He resumes work on his wreath.

The kid grabs something from Steve's desk.

                  STEVE (CONT'D)
        You just took my teasel!

                    KID
          So if I did?

Steve clocks him.

The two fall to the floor between the desks,
wrestling, taking boxes of flowers down with them.
Everyone come rushing to watch.

                    MISS GRAVES
          Boys! Boys!

Steve and his team-mate scuffle among the flowers.
It isn't pretty.

                                   FADE OUT:

EXT. JUNIOR BOYS REPUBLIC (COURTYARD) -- DAY

A banner hangs across the entrance: **Merry Christmas
1945!**

Steve gazes at cars filled with happy-looking boys
driving off with their parents.

                    BOY
          Merry Christmas McQueer!

                    STEVE
          Watch out your sister doesn't
          catch you under the mistletoe!

Steve shares a threatening glance with one of his
team-mates going off with his mother.

                                   DISSOLVE TO:

EXT. JUNIOR BOYS REPUBLIC (GROUNDS) -- LATER

The day wears on. Steve wanders the deserted
grounds. The only soul in sight.

EXT. JUNIOR BOYS REPUBLIC (COURTYARD) -- LATER

Later, he sits on a chair staring at the front
gates, rocking back and forth.

INT. JUNIOR BOYS REPUBLIC (CABIN) -- CONTINUOUS

Steve enters his cabin, opening the door, but he
can no longer contain his rage: he slams the door
half-a-dozen times until it comes off its hinges.

He overturns his bed and collapses on the mattress,
sobbing.

Alone.

EXT. JUNIOR BOYS REPUBLIC (FRANK GRAVES HOUSE) --
EVENING

Frank Graves parks his car in front of an
unassuming bungalow.

Steve is in the passenger seat, solemn and red eyed.

At the front door, they're greeted by Miss Graves.

                    MISS GRAVES
          I'm so glad you'll be joining us
          for dinner.

She extends a welcoming hand. Steve stares at her,
grim.

                    STEVE
          Ma'am.

INT. FRANK GRAVES HOUSE (DINING ROOM) -- NIGHT

A sumptuous turkey is at the heart of the table.
Miss Graves serves.

                    MISS GRAVES
          Eggnog, dear?

Steve looks at her like she's asked him a question
in math class.

INT. FRANK GRAVES HOUSE (DINING ROOM) -- LATER

They're eating. Silence. Hardly festive.

Miss Graves shares a glance with her husband.

                    FRANK GRAVES
          Look Steve, we all have to learn
          how to compromise—

Steve glares over his turkey.

                    FRANK GRAVES (CONT'D)
          Life doesn't always deal out an
          even hand, but it's how we play
          the cards we've been dealt—

                    STEVE
               (muttered under his
               breath while eating)
          That's bullsh—

                    MISS GRAVES
                   (over Steve)
          I don't think a gambling
          metaphor is very appropriate,
          dear.

Frank Graves remains focused on Steve.

                    FRANK GRAVES
          You could be somebody special,
          Steve. Give life an honest shot.

Steve studies his headmaster, surprised he
genuinely cares.

                                        CUT TO:

INT. BUS -- DAY

Steve's on a bus driving cross country.

                    FRANK GRAVES (O.S.)
          We received a letter from your
          mother.

He glances out the window, watching the Midwest
landscape slide by.

                    FRANK GRAVES (O.S.) (CONT'D)
          Go on. Open it.

Steve watches another passenger unwrap a sandwich.

                    FRANK GRAVES (O.S.) (CONT'D)
          What does she have to say?

EXT. BUS -- DAY

The highway speeds beneath the wheels of the bus
and its chrome bumper.

> STEVE (O.S.)
> My stepfather's dead. She wants
> me to go to New York.

INT. BUS -- DAY

Steve turns away from the window.

CUT TO:

EXT. MONTAGE SEQUENCE

Red stands by his biplane, his face obscured in
shadow. He climbs into the cockpit.

DISSOLVE to Steve as a young boy running on his
uncle's farm...

...followed by his mother tenderly looking at him
in the back of Berri's car when she first picked
him up.

INT. BUS -- DAY

Groggy, Steve wakes from his dream and peers
outside.

INT / EXT. NEW YORK -- DAY

The streets of New York float by, reflected in the
window's glass.

EXT. BUS DEPOT -- DAY

Steve gets off the bus. There's no one to greet him.

INT. BUS DEPOT -- DAY

He enters Central Station. Still no sign of his mother.

Steve glances at the overhead clock. 4:30PM.

                                        CUT TO:

INT. MONTAGE SEQUENCE

Jump cuts show Steve sitting on a bench.

Browsing the newspapers.

Sleeping on the bench.

Swiping a soda. The shadows grow long.

INT. BUS DEPOT -- NIGHT

He looks at the clock. 11PM.

Frustrated, he grabs his bags and defiantly makes for the exit.

EXT. BUS DEPOT -- NIGHT

Steve stands on the street corner.

                    JULLIAN
          Steve!? Steven!

He turns and sees his mother hurrying up the street,
frantically waving her hand. Tailing her is a
Bohemian guy in his forties, VICTOR LUKENS. Steve's
relieved, but barely forces a smile.

EXT. NEW YORK APARTMENT -- NIGHT

Steve stands with Jullian in front of a brownstone
apartment.

His mother holds up a key.

>   JULLIAN
>   Your very own place. Victor and
>   me are right upstairs.
>   (she hesitates)
>   I'm sorry 'bout not comin' to
>   see you... you know, with Berri
>   an' all. Victor's different.

Steve nods and accepts the key. He descends to the
subbasement apartment.

>   JULLIAN (CONT'D)
>   I'm sure you'll get along with
>   your room-mate.

INT. NEW YORK BASEMENT APARTMENT (LIVING ROOM /
KITCHEN & BEDROOM)-- NIGHT

Steve enters the dark basement apartment.
Streetlight gleams through the barred window. He
flicks the switch.

It's a dive.

Steve throws his luggage aside and explores.
There's leftover food on the kitchen table &
cigarette butts. In the fridge, there's nothing but
Coors and cake.

Clothing strewn on the floor leads to the single
bedroom.

He opens the door—

—and sees in the shadows two naked men, startled
out of bed.

For a moment, Steve stares at them: one of the guys
clings to the other. As soon as the shock wares off,
Steve beelines for the exit.

> ROOMMATE
> Shit! It's Jullian's kid. I
> thought he was comin' tomorrow!

INT. NEW YORK APARTMENT (JULLIAN'S FLAT) -- NIGHT

Steve barges into his mother's room.

> STEVE
> Thanks for nothing, I'm leaving.

Lukens shares a knowing glance with Jullian.

> JULLIAN
> Oh, c'mon, grow up! You think
> everyone's like you?

Seething, Steve heads for the door.

> JULLIAN (CONT'D)
> This's a rough city and you're
> just a kid.

Steve opens the door.

> JULLIAN (CONT'D)
> If you leave, don't come back!

Steve looks at her one last time.

> STEVE
> I won't be coming back.

He goes out.

EXT. NEW YORK STREETS -- NIGHT

Steve hurries down the street in the pouring rain, holding his jacket over his head.

INT. NEW YORK BAR -- NIGHT

Looking like a drenched rat, Steve enters a seedy bar. He sidles up to the counter, catching the bartender's attention.

> STEVE
> Hey, man. I'm broke. I'll do the
> dishes or whatever for something
> to eat.

> BARTENDER
> I ain't a charity. Find
> someplace else, alright?

Dejected, Steve heads for the exit.

Two merchant sailors seated at a table, FORD and TINKER, take notice.

                    FORD
          Hey, kid! Kid! We're not all
          assholes in New York. Grab a
          seat.

Reluctant, Steve sits: no other choice.

                    FORD (CONT'D)
          Have a drink.

He pushes a bottle in front of Steve. Dying of
thirst, Steve accepts.

                    FORD (CONT'D)
          Let me guess. Lookin' for a
          little adventure?

Steve takes a swig of beer.

                                        CUT TO:

EXT. S.S. ALPHA (AT SEA) -- DAY

A rusting, beat-up, barely seaworthy tanker sways
in the endless ocean. The sky is crystal blue.

INT / EXT. S.S. ALPHA (AT SEA) -- DAY

Steve groans, draped over a bed of duffel bags on
deck, sleeping.

                    OFFICER (O.S.)
          Crewman! You there!?

Steve raises a hand to block out the glaring sun.
He's got a massive hangover.

                    STEVE
          What time is it?

                    OFFICER
        Time for you to get to work!
        'Fore I throw you overboard!

                    STEVE
        Where am I? Where's the bus?

                    OFFICER
        Yonkers is that way!

He points over the ocean.

Steve sits up and looks around.

                    STEVE
               (remembering)
        Where're we?

                    OFFICER
        Headed West Indies. With a
        boatload of molasses to cover
        your mama's pancakes from here
        to the moon. Now bust your ass!

INT / EXT. S.S. ALPHA (AT SEA) -- DAY

Steve swabs the deck, watching others go about
their work aboard the tanker.

                                        CUT TO:

Steve empties a trash can over the side. He leans
across the railing, watching the garbage splash in
the Atlantic.

Surprisingly, he's happy, filled with a sense of
freedom.

INT / EXT. S.S. ALPHA (AT SEA) -- NIGHT

Night descends on the S.S. Alpha. The sky is
crimson.

INT. S.S. ALPHA (CORRIDOR) -- NIGHT

It's dark in the bowels of the ship. Two
flashlights play along the humid bulkhead. Tinker
and Ford appear to be lost.

                   FORD
      Are we in the right section?

                  TINKER
      McQueen said A-203.

Ford bangs his head.

                   FORD
      Fuck! Who turned out the lights?

He rubs his forehead.

               FORD (CONT'D)
      Why'd he want us to come?

                  TINKER
      How should I know? I thought he
      told you.

                   FORD
      Me? I thought you knew. Where is
      that beanpole?

                  TINKER
      Here it is.

Tinker shines his flashlight on a door.

Ford opens it and steps through, when his foot
catches a trip wire.

A pail over the door tips, dumping a slew of
garbage on him.

> FORD
> What the hell?!

From across the room, Steve emerges, laughing and
holding his belly.

> STEVE
> Don't move! I gotta get a photo
> of this! Anyone got a camera?

Ford wipes himself.

> FORD
> What's that smell?!

Tinker's laughing too.

> TINKER
> Oh, sweet Jesus, Mary of shit!

He steps to the door and looks up at the elaborate
rig.

> TINKER (CONT'D)
> Quite a setup—

—He accidentally trips the wire again.

Garbage plops onto his upturned face.

Steve and Ford crack up.

> FORD
> You walked right into it!

                    STEVE
          What an idiot—

                    TINKER
          Your balls are mine, McQueen!

An officer happens across them.

                    OFFICER
          What's this goddamn mess?!!

The three look like chastised children.

                                        CUT TO:

INT / EXT. S.S. ALPHA (AT SEA) -- EVENING

Seagulls swirl overhead.

Steve, Ford and Tinker have found a quiet corner to
themselves, playing cards on deck.

                    FORD
          Three Jacks.

                    TINKER
          Shiiit, man.

Ford clears the pot of money.

                    FORD
          Your deal.

Steve deals the cards.

                    FORD (CONT'D)
          So, kid, how'd you end up in New
          York?

                    STEVE
     I was supposed to meet up with
     my ma, but I changed my mind.

Ford and Tinker study him, when—

                    OFFICER (O.S.)
          Fire!

The klaxon blares. Everything turns to chaos;
crewmen run past.

INT / EXT. S.S. ALPHA (AT SEA) -- MOMENTS LATER

Steve, Ford and Tinker arrive by a cabin with
flames shooting out the window. They watch,
fascinated, as if staring at a car accident.

The tanker sways in heavy seas.

                    CREWMAN
          The pumps are jammed!

Steve sees some crew members holding a fire-hose.
An officer twists the tap to no effect. The First
Officer is standing behind Steve:

                    FIRST OFFICER
          Surrounded by ocean and we've
          got no fuckin' water!

Steve watches the commotion.

                    STEVE
          The ballast tanks are full,
          ain't they?

The First Officer glances at Steve: is it a good
idea?

CUT TO:

INT. S.S. ALPHA (HOLD) -- NIGHT

In the depths of the ship, a line of crewmen are formed in front of a spout protruding from a pipe.

Water pours into buckets and the crewmen pass the buckets down the line — along the corridor —

and up metal stairs.

INT / EXT. S.S. ALPHA (AT SEA) -- NIGHT

The bucket is passed from hand to hand along deck. Sweating crewmen are silhouetted against the dark sea.

A bucket lands in Steve's hands and he throws water on the raging fire. He's exhilarated: life and death!

Finally:

> OFFICER
> We've got power!

Spray shoots from the repaired fire-house, dousing the flames.

Steve mops his soot covered forehead, exhausted... yet smiling.

CUT TO:

EXT. HARBOR -- MORNING

The S.S. Alpha sails into harbor under calm seas.

A subtitle reads: **Dominican Republic, 1946.**

EXT. DOCKS -- DAY

The docks are bustling with workers.

Steve stealthily pushes his way through, glancing back at the docked tanker one last time, before melting into the crowd.

EXT. BOARDWALK -- NIGHT

Overlooking the wharves, Steve wanders the boardwalk at night.

A dark-skinned beauty idling by the railing catches his eye.

> PROSTITUE
> Hey, Sailor! *Brechador!*

Steve takes in her long legs.

INT. BROTHEL -- NIGHT

With the prostitute hanging onto his arm, Steve enters a brothel. He's all smiles and she laughs at something he whispers into her ear. She stops by the stairs.

> PROSTITUE
> *Esta bien,* but you pay first.

                              STEVE
          I thought we had something
          special.

                            PROSTITUE
          No, no, you pay first.

                              STEVE
          Man, I just got out to sea. No
          paycheck, comprendo?

                            PROSTITUE
          Tacano! Then go home sailor,
          back to U.S.A.!

                              STEVE
          Alright, forget it — Just forget
          it!

Steve heads for the door, shoulders slumped.

                            PROSTITUE
          Hey—

Steve turns back to her.

                       PROSTITUE (CONT'D)
          Arrecho? Ever been with a *chica
          rapana*?

Steve doesn't answer.

                       PROSTITUE (CONT'D)
          Ever been with anyone?

                                              CUT TO:

INT. BROTHEL (ROOM) -- NIGHT

Steve, awkward, makes love with the prostitute, her
dark skin glistening.

The Latin sounds of the city drift through the
curtained windows.

                                                CUT TO:

EXT. SANTO DOMINGO STREET -- DAY

Happy as a clam and now wearing local clothing,
Steve weaves through a fruit market, grabbing a
papaya from a stand. He knows his way around town.

                                                CUT TO:

INT. BROTHEL (ROOM) -- DAY

Steve shakes out a bed-sheet, changing the linen.

INT. BROTHEL (HALLWAY) -- DAY

As Steve exits with an armful of clean sheets,
ready for the next room, he sees a balding, middle-
aged Hispanic man come out of it.

Steve enters.

INT. BROTHEL (ROOM) -- DAY

A dark eyed beauty is counting money by the window,
naked.

Steve changes the pillowcases. The prostitute
watches.

                    2ND PROSTITUTE
          Bacano — there's a shortage of
          blond men around here...

Steve, reserved —trying to ignore her nakedness—
glances her way and shrugs.

                    2ND PROSTITUTE (CONT'D)
          Had a chance to sample the rest
          of the wares?

Steve drinks her sight in. She smiles. He throws
his armful of bed-sheets aside.

EXT/INT. BROTHEL -- NIGHT

The rowdy, twinkling city of Santo Domingo at night
lies beneath Steve's feet. He's seated on a balcony,
counting money from an envelope.

                    PROSTITUE (O.S.)
          Sometimes I feel we should be
          paying you more.

She stands in the doorway by the billowing curtain.

                    STEVE
          S'alright. Got me enough.

                    PROSTITUE
          Enough for what?

                    STEVE
          To go home.

She studies him thoughtfully.

                    PROSTITUE
          And where is your home?

But Steve doesn't have an answer.

                                        CUT TO:

EXT. HARBOR -- MORNING

Steve's haggling with a fishmonger.

                    STEVE
          Dos Pesos! Dos Pesos!

The fishmonger holds up his fingers, three pesos!
Steve stuffs two bills into the proffered hand.

                    STEVE (CONT'D)
          Dos Pesos, Amigo!

Steve selects a fish. Grudgingly, the fishmonger
wraps it up.

INT. BROTHEL -- MORNING

Steve enters the brothel with his parcel, when—

                    PROSTITUE (O.S.)
                (shrill scream)
          Socorro! Atacante!

He races upstairs.

INT. BROTHEL (HALLWAY) -- MORNING

                    PROSTITUE (O.S.)
          Socorro!

Steve barges through the door.

INT. BROTHEL (ROOM) -- MORNING

And stops in his tracks.

The prostitute he first met is lying on the bed,
pretending to be ravished, while a man calmly gets
undressed.

> PROSTITUE
>> *Socorro—*

She sees Steve.

> CLIENT
>> Who're you?

Steve grabs the man by the arm.

> STEVE
>> Whadaya think you're doing!?

> PROSTITUE
>> No, no Steve — it's ok.

> CLIENT
>> What is this?

> PROSTITUE
>> I'm ok.

> STEVE
>> It's not ok.

> CLIENT
>> We're just havin' some fun. It
>> look like I'm raping her?

Steve lets go of the man and glances at the girl.
She nods, embarrassed.

                    CLIENT (CONT'D)
          Now you gone and broke the mood.

He grabs his money off the bed.

                    PROSTITUE
          Honey—

                    CLIENT
          Some other time. When there's no
          crazy American come bustin' in.

He slams out. Steve turns to the prostitute, but on
seeing her, feels ashamed for his actions.

                    PROSTITUE
          What're you sticking around here
          for? You think this is your
          dream?

                                    SMASH CUT TO:

EXT. OIL RIG -- DAY

A subtitle reads: **Port Arthur, Texas.**

Steve, shirtless, is smeared in oil and wearing a
hard-hat.

He's working on an oil rig.

                    WORKER
          C'mon, Steve. We don't have all
          day!

Steve connects a cable to a large pipe, swinging it
through the air.

                    STEVE
          I'm just a spec o' dirt under
          the totem pole of this here rig.

78

                    WORKER
        You wish you were dirt. Dirt's
        got it easier. Dirt ain't gotta
        work so it can eat.

                    STEVE
                  (smiling)
        Bush-man salute!

He waves the flies away, in half-imitation of an
army salute.

The others laugh.

                                        CUT TO:

EXT. COUNTRY HIGHWAY -- DAY

Steve stands on a highway shoulder.

He sticks out his thumb.

                                        CUT TO:

EXT. ANOTHER COUNTRY HIGHWAY -- DAY

Steve's left off at an intersection by the car that
picked him up.

                    STEVE
        Thanks, buddy.

Once again, he tries to hitch a ride.

No one stops.

Finally, a beatnik on a motorbike pulls up. This is
HAROLD.

> HAROLD
> Where you headed, man?

> STEVE
> Where you going?

> HAROLD
> Looks like your way.

EXT. MOTORBIKE / HIGHWAY -- DAY

Steve clings to the back of Harold's bike. Pure
freedom.

EXT. GAS STATION -- DAY

Harold stops at a gas station where they dismount
to stretch.

> STEVE
> Why don't you take a break and
> let me drive?

EXT. MOTORBIKE / HIGHWAY -- DAY

Moving at breakneck speeds, Harold clings to Steve
for dear life.

They pass a sign, "Welcome to South Carolina".

Zooming along a single-lane country highway, Steve
weaves in and out of traffic, barely avoiding head
on collisions.

                    HAROLD
              (over the wind)
        Slow down! My bike can't take
        it!

                    STEVE
        I can't hear you!

                                        CUT TO:

EXT. HIGHWAY SHOULDER -- DAY

Broken down, the bike is by the side of the road
with Harold flat on his back trying to fix it.

                    HAROLD
        I told you, man.
              (louder)
        Did I say I told you?

Steve stands a few paces away, idly twisting a
piece of straw in his mouth.

                    STEVE
        You might' a.

Harold continues to grumble, while Steve glances up
and down the highway.

A car is approaching.

It's an open-topped vehicle with three girls. They
slow down.

                    FEMALE DRIVER
        Hey there, need a hand?

Steve spots the girl in back, a beautiful red-head
with green eyes; austere and confident. This is SUE
ANN.

                    STEVE
        S'okay. We're alright.

A sudden gust of wind blows off Sue Ann's hat.

Steve stoops, grabs it and hands it back. Their
eyes lock.

Steve remains trained on Sue Ann, who smiles at him,
intrigued... The other girls snicker.

                    FEMALE DRIVER
        Be seeing yah.

The girls giggle, driving away.

Steve rubs his neck, considering. He marches over
to Harold.

                    STEVE
        Move over.

Steve glances at the engine, fiddles with something,
then mounts the bike. After one or two throttles,
it purrs to life.

                    HAROLD
        What'd you do—?

But Steve isn't waiting around; Harold jumps on.

                                        CUT TO:

EXT. HIGHWAY -- DAY

Steve zooms through lush, green countryside.

As the highway twists and turns through the trees,
he loses sight of the girls' car.

He slows at an intersection.

> STEVE
> Which way'd they go?

> HAROLD
> Which way'd who go? Those
> girls?!

Steve ignores him and turns the bike around.

At the next cross-street he stops, deciding which
way looks more promising.

> HAROLD (CONT'D)
> Where you headed, man?!

Steve turns down one of the streets.

EXT. GENTRIFIED NEIGHBORHOOD -- EVENING

Steve drives through a neighborhood with large
mansions on either side.

He slows, soaking in the impressive houses: this is
the life for him!

> HAROLD
> Keep your eyes on the road!

EXT. TOWN OF MYRTLE BEACH -- EVENING

With the last mansion behind them, Steve passes a
sign: "Myrtle Beach"

He stops on the outskirts of town and gets off.

                    STEVE
          Thanks for the ride.

                    HAROLD
          Look man, I hope you find
          whatever it is you're looking
          for.

                    STEVE
          Yeah. Me too.

They shake, then Harold turns around, back the way
they came.

The town is deserted.

Steve wanders down a lane, toward the beach front,
alone.

EXT. MYRTLE BEACH -- NIGHT

He stares at the ocean, lost in his thoughts.

From the reeds, a crane rises and swoops across the
night sky.

EXT. BEACH PATH -- NIGHT

Steve wanders along a path away from the beach.

                                        CUT TO:

EXT. TOWN OF MYRTLE BEACH -- MORNING

A scruffy looking Steve roams tiredly along the
sidewalk.

Shop-owners are opening for the day.

Steve stops, glancing in a store window. TV sets are for sale.

He notices a sign: *help wanted.*

CUT TO:

EXT. MANSION -- DAY

A rusting jeep is parked outside an impressive beach-front mansion. Steve lugs a brand new set out of the back of the vehicle.

EXT / INT. MANSION -- DAY

At the entrance, he's greeted by a fashionable woman in her forties, LINDA.

> LINDA
> Oh, finally it's here. Can you bring it into the living room?

> STEVE
> Sure. Make no never mind.

He follows her into the living room.

Through glass patio doors, Steve notices someone sunbathing.

He can only discern a large, trendy hat above the lawn chair, and the glimmer of a raised, slender leg.

> LINDA
> Just set it here.

Steve places the TV.

                    LINDA (CONT'D)
        Do you know how to turn it on?
        I'm so helpless with these
        things.

Steve plugs in the TV. He fiddles with the rabbit
ears until a crisp, black and white image appears.

                    LINDA (CONT'D)
        That's simply spectacular. It's
        amazing, isn't it?

Steve nods.

                    LINDA (CONT'D)
                 (calling)
        Sue Ann, dear. Come see this.
        Sue Ann—

Steve turns and sees the girl on the patio rise
from her lawn chair. It's Sue Ann in a trim bathing
suit.

She stands next to her mother and Steve, affecting
not to recognize him.

                    SUE ANN
        Hi.

All three stare at the TV. A Western is playing.

                    LINDA
        What won't they think of next?

Sue Ann sneaks a glance at Steve, who's too shy to
look at her. She smiles inwardly.

                    SUE ANN
        I'll be outside.

She turns, brushing Steve's shoulder on her way to the patio.

> STEVE
> If you'll excuse me ma'am, I've other deliveries.

> LINDA
> Alright.

Steve (wanting to catch up with Sue Ann) hurries to the front door, when—

> LINDA (CONT'D)
> Oh — I forgot to pay! How silly of me.

She counts out the money; Steve can barely stand still.

EXT. MANSION / BEACH -- DAY

Steve hurries around the side of the house.

But as he nears the beach, he freezes. What to do?

Sue Ann calmly walks along the shore, bending to pick up some shells.

She watches a sand-crab dig a hole, before looking up, noticing Steve frozen by the side of the house. She smiles.

Regaining his nerve, Steve plucks a wild-flower growing nearby. He marches purposefully toward the beach.

                        STEVE
            Here. This is for you.

She studies him for a moment, letting Steve suffer
in his awkwardness. She takes the flower, laughing
out loud despite herself.

                        SUE ANN
            I don't even know your name.

He sticks out his hand.

                        STEVE
            Steve — McQueen.

Sue Ann accepts his hand. She laughs.

                        SUE ANN
            Sue Ann.

Still holding hands:

                        STEVE
            I was wondering if you'd like to
            go out with me?

                        SUE ANN
            Now? Why? Go with you...?
                (she laughs)

                        STEVE
            Tomorrow. Around six o'clock?

Sue Ann smiles. Radiant.

Reluctant, Steve lets go of her hand.

Sue Ann watches him walk away, glancing down at the
meager flower. Her green eyes twinkle.

                                              CUT TO:

EXT. JEEP -- DAY

Steve drives the jeep, happy as can be.

INT. SODA SHOP -- NIGHT

Steve, by himself, is eating a burger. He watches
people come and go. Even alone, he's happy —
thinking of Sue Ann.

                                            FADE OUT:

INT. TV STORE -- DAY

Steve glances into a room at the back of the TV
shop. An elderly man is tinkering with an open set.

                    STEVE
          I'm gonna borrow the jalopy
          tonight.

                    STORE OWNER
          Uh-huh.

                                              CUT TO:

EXT. MANSION -- EVENING

Steve rings the doorbell. He's in a shirt and jeans,
rumpled looking. The door opens.

                    SUE ANN
          Hi—?

Sue Ann's wearing a lovely white gown. She glances
dubiously at Steve in his jeans. Ignoring her
expression, Steve drags Sue Ann to the jeep.

                        STEVE
          C'mon. You look good.

                                        CUT TO:

INT / EXT. JEEP -- NIGHT

Sue Ann sits next to Steve as they drive along a
country road.

                        STEVE
              You know, I figured I'd never
              stack up with the other clams if
              we did the usual shin-dig.

                        SUE ANN
          What did you have in mind?

Without warning, Steve veers off the road. Sue Ann
screeches.

EXT. BEACH -- NIGHT

The jeep bounds over a dune in Thomas Crown style
before coming to a halt.

INT / EXT. JEEP -- NIGHT

Steve's smiling gleefully.

He turns to Sue Ann.

For an instant, she's rigid. She puts her hand to
her chest, feeling the thump of her heart. Then
she turns to Steve and breaks into laughter.

                         SUE ANN
          My heart's beating a mile a
          minute!

                         STEVE
          Hold on.

He guns the jeep. It takes off through the sand.

EXT. BEACH -- NIGHT

The jeep roars across the beach into the surf,
sending up a spray of water.

Sue Ann stands with her hands balanced on the
jeep's windshield.

INT / EXT. JEEP -- NIGHT

                         SUE ANN
          Wooo!!!!

Steve smiles intently.

EXT. BEACH -- NIGHT

The jeep glides through the surf in the reflection
of the moonlight.

                                        CUT TO:

EXT. MANSION -- NIGHT

The jeep halts in front of the mansion. Sue Ann
bounds to the front door — no time to kiss.

                         SUE ANN
          I had a great time.

                    STEVE
        When can I see you again?

INT. MANSION (DINING ROOM) - ANOTHER DAY

Steve squirms at dinner in a new suit: a fish out
of water.

He doesn't know which silverware to choose.

                    LINDA
        So Steve, why don't you tell us
        about yourself?

Steve stares blankly at Sue Ann's parents,
grandmother, and kid brother.

                    STEVE
        Uh, I — Uhm.

                    SUE ANN
        What about your travels? Steve's
        seen so many exciting things.

                    LINDA
        From what we've heard, it sounds
        like you had quite the adventure.

                    STEVE
        Well... I guess I feel I've
        learned more by seein' the world
        than from any musty, ol'
        textbook.
                (catching himself)
        Not that book-learnin' ain't
        important.
                (he points his fork
                at her kid brother)
        So, stay in school, y'hear?

                    LINDA
        What did your mother say about
        you going off like that?

The question hits Steve in the gut.

                    SUE ANN
        You don't have to answer. We
        don't mean to pry.

                    NANA
        Of course we mean to pry. Why
        else did we invite him?

                    SUE ANN
        Nana!

                    LINDA
        Now settle down. In this country,
        what counts most is where you're
        headed, not where you're from.

                    NANA
        What twat—

                    LINDA
        Perry, will you tell your
        mother—

                    PERRY
        Linda, please don't abuse my
        mother.

                    SUE ANN
        I'm sorry about this, Steve.

                    STEVE
        No, it's alright. They're
        justified to wonder 'bout my
        intentions.

                    NANA
          So the boy's got sense after all.

The soup is served. Sue Ann's father interjects:

                    PERRY
          And just what is the family
          business you "skipped out on" to
          see the world?

Steve pretends not to hear, slurping his soup
loudly.

The rest of the family share an uncertain glance.

                    STEVE
          Delicious soup.

                                        CUT TO:

INT. MANSION -- EVENING

Sue Ann slides dirty bowls into the sink. Her
mother follows.

                    SUE ANN
          What do you think?

Her mother hesitates.

                    LINDA
          ...He's very handsome.
               (beat)
          And dirt poor.

                    SUE ANN
          We haven't even gotten to the
          main course, and you all can't
          wait to show him the door.

94

                    LINDA
              (as an afterthought)
          He is very handsome.

INT. MANSION (DINING ROOM) -- EVENING

They return to the dining room, but Steve's chair
is empty.

                    SUE ANN
              Where's Steve?

                    NANA
              Boy can't hold his bladder.

Sue Ann's father eats noisily.

                                        CUT TO:

INT. BATHROOM -- EVENING

Steve flushes, wiping the perspiration from his
brow. He's amazed at all the fancy towels.

INT. MANSION (DINING ROOM) -- EVENING

                    SUE ANN
              (to her father)
          What about you? You don't like
          him either.

                    PERRY
          I didn't say anything.

                    NANA
          Your father is being judicious.

                    SUE ANN
You won't even give him a
chance—

                    NANA
Thank god I never had a daughter.

                    LINDA
Honey, we're just being
realistic.

                    SUE ANN
He works. He has a job.

                    PERRY
And you expect to live off a TV
repairman's salary?

Steve, standing at the back of the dining room, has
overheard the last bit.

                    STEVE
I only deliver 'em, sir.

                                        CUT TO:

EXT. MANSION -- NIGHT

Steve stands on the front porch with Sue Ann and
her parents.

                    STEVE
It, it was a — a evening. I mean,
it was nice to make your
acquaintance—

                    PERRY
          Steve, you seem like a hard-
          working young man, which is more
          than can be said for most of the
          silver-spoon-fed self-entitled
          brats who come calling on our
          daughter.

                    SUE ANN
          Dad!

Her father holds up a key, indicating the gleaming
car in the driveway.

                    PERRY
          Have a good evening.

EXT. CHURCH PARKING LOT -- NIGHT

Light and music streams from a church.

INT. CHURCH (DANCE HALL) -- NIGHT

Steve enters the dance hall arm-in-arm with Sue Ann,
noticing the glances cast their way from curious
onlookers.

                    SUE ANN
          If anyone asks, I'll say you're
          the son of one of my father's
          business associates. An out-of-
          towner.

                    STEVE
          Sure.

                    SUE ANN
        Did I just insult you? I didn't
        mean to. But if you're going to
        fit in with this crowd, you
        learn pretty quick to have a
        thick skin.

                    STEVE
        It make no never mind.

Steve and Sue Ann slow dance, at a respectful
distance.

He jealously glances at the other well-heeled
couples, then at Sue Ann... who inches closer and
rests her head on his shoulder.

They dance.

                                        CUT TO:

INT. MOVIE PALACE -- DAY

Steve and Sue Ann huddle watching a James Cagney
movie.

                    "WHITE HEAT"
                (on screen)
        Always thinking about your Cody,
        aren't you?
                (more)
        That's right.
                (more)
        Top of the world, son.
                (more)
        Don't know what I'd do without
        you, Ma.
                (more)
        Now go on out. Show them you're
        all right.

Sue Ann grips Steve's arm: he's completely engrossed.

EXT. MOVIE PALACE -- LATER

Steve and Sue Ann exit the movie theater into the blinding sun.

He raises his arm to block the glare, still entranced by the Cagney flick.

> SUE ANN
> Hey, c'mon. Remember the real
> world?

EXT. MANSION -- DAY

Steve stops by the front door with Sue Ann.

> SUE ANN
> Why don't you come in for a
> minute?

> STEVE
> I don't think your folks have
> taken much of a shine to me.

> SUE ANN
> Oh, don't be a spoilsport.

INT. MANSION -- DAY

She leads him through the front hall, when—

> FAMILY
> Surprise!!!

Sue Ann's mother appears with a birthday cake and candles.

The family sings *Happy Birthday Steve*...

Steve beams, blushing.

CUT TO:

EXT / INT. STABLES / FIELD -- DAY

Steve's frowning.

He's saddling up a horse. Some friends of Sue Ann's are already mounted, outside the stable.

Sue Ann joins him.

>   SUE ANN
>   Why're you being such a dead
>   beat?

>   STEVE
>   You told 'em I'm a sailor.

>   SUE ANN
>   So?

>   STEVE
>   It wasn't that kind of boat.

Steve strokes his horse.

>   SUE ANN
>   If you'd give them a chance,
>   you'll see they're not so bad.

Steve nods and mounts.

He shoots out of the stable.

DERRICK, a preppie jock, spurs his horse to catch up, followed by the girls.

They fall into a trot.

> DERRICK
> Got a good horse there, Steve.
> Good color. Palomino. English
> saddle's much more refined,
> don't you think?

> STEVE
> — Couldn't agree —

Derrick looks taken aback.

> STEVE (CONT'D)
> I mean, I couldn't agree more.

The four of them ride in silence.

> DERRICK
> See those vineyards? My father's
> bottling Merlot. It takes a
> special winemaker to give it
> that full-body taste, not too
> woody, and just a little fruity.

> STEVE
> Well, like father like son.

> DERRICK
> I'll take that as a compliment.

> STEVE
> (under his breath)
> Fruity.

He breaks into a gallop, racing ahead.

CUT TO:

EXT. BLUFF OVERLOOKING OCEAN -- DUSK

Steve and Sue Ann walk along a bluff, a high cliff
overlooking crashing waves. Steve, morose, totters
along the edge.

Sue Ann, fearful, remains a few paces back.

                    SUE ANN
          I wish you wouldn't do that.

Steve glances at the rocks far below.

She pulls him by the arm, away from the ledge.

                    STEVE
          I'm just a hick from a pig farm.

                    SUE ANN
          You're so much smarter than
          those clowns.

                    STEVE
          They'll never stop laughin'
          behind my back.

                    SUE ANN
          What are you saying?

                    STEVE
          I don't know.

                    SUE ANN
          Steve....

                    STEVE
          We ain't really cut out for each
          other.

Sue Ann watches his stern back, her heart breaking.

                    SUE ANN
          Do you love me?

He turns away, facing the surf.

                    SUE ANN (CONT'D)
                  (tearful)
          Steve, do you love me?!

                    STEVE
          Don't ask me 'bout that.

                    SUE ANN
          Why not? Because no one's ever
          loved you before?

                    STEVE
          I don't need anyone's love.

Steve stares at the waves.

                                        CUT TO:

INT. TV STORE -- NIGHT

In the corner of the TV store, hidden among half a
dozen sets, Steve shows Sue Ann the cot where he's
been sleeping.

                    STEVE
          This's where I've been...
          stayin'.

Sue Ann sits on the cot, uncertain what to make of
it all.

Through an overhead window she notices the
brilliant stars.

The stars glitter, reflected on the TVs behind her.

                    SUE ANN
        It's beautiful.

                    STEVE
        I feel like I've fallen into a
        dream... but it's not real.

Steve sits at the foot of the bed.

                    STEVE (CONT'D)
        I thought it over. I'm enlisting.

She sits up — and kisses him.

                    SUE ANN
        Don't worry about me.

                    STEVE
        I promise I'll come back.

EXT. BOOT CAMP -- DAY

The camera pulls back from a sign: Camp Lejeune,
revealing Steve exiting a school bus among a line
of recruits.

INT. BOOT CAMP (RECEPTION) -- DAY

An officer stamps a form: cadet #649015, handing it
to Steve, who moves to the next line to get his
physical.

INT. BOOT CAMP (PHYSICAL EXAM) -- DAY

A doctor checks out Steve. He holds a tuning fork
to his ear.

The *hummmm* is audible.

> DOCTOR
> Hear that?

> STEVE
> Yes sir.

The doc holds it to Steve's other ear.

No sound.

> DOCTOR
> And that?

> STEVE
> Just fine.

CUT TO:

INT. MANSION (SUE ANN'S BEDROOM) -- NIGHT

Sue Ann sits at her night-table and composes a letter.

EXT. BOOT CAMP -- MORNING

Steve's lugging laundry baskets in shirt sleeves from the officer's quarters. Grunt work.

> SUE ANN (V.O.)
> Steve, I know it's only been a
> week, but I miss you already.
> You're different from the other
> boys. We're all very proud
> you're in the marines.

EXT. BOOT CAMP -- DAY

Steve, smirking mirthfully, runs away from the open engine of a jeep where he'd been working, when some other soldiers walk past.

A heated can of beans explodes, catching the soldiers!

> SUE ANN (V.O.)
> I'm thrilled to hear you're
> settling into your regiment and
> doing well. My brother's always
> playing army. He really looks up
> to you.

INT. BOOT CAMP (BUNK) -- DAY

Steve stands with a raised beer can while his bunkmates lazily watch:

> STEVE
> Men, never forget your rights!
> We have the right to drink, get
> laid, race bikes and tool
> around!

The others laugh.

EXT. BOOT CAMP -- DAY

Steve shoots off some rounds for a training exercise. Bull's-eye!

His superior officer frowns when he sees Steve's put up a photo of him on the target.

                    SUE ANN (V.O.)
          I told my mother you're being
          considered for promotion. I
          hope we'll see each other soon,
          but don't worry, I know your
          duty comes first.

INT. BOOT CAMP (OFFICE) -- DAY

A Seargeant is in Steve's face:

                    SEARGANT
          McQueen, the only way you'll
          make corporal is if all the
          other privates in the Marines
          drop dead!

Steve remains stone faced under the Sergeant's
withering glare.

                    SEARGANT (CONT'D)
          I'm transferring you to the
          Second Division of the Fleet
          Marine Force—

EXT. MILITARY LOT -- DAY

                    SEARGANT (V.O.)
          —Where I hope you'll make
          yourself useful!

Steve walks among a row of tanks, glancing at the
"report for duty" order in hand.

                    STEVE
          PFC McQueen reporting for duty,
          sir!

The head-officer hands back the papers.

                    DUTY OFFICER
          Alright McQueen, dump your
          duffel and see if you can't help
          us with this—

                    STEVE
          Sure.

One of the soldiers working on the tank looks up
and recognizes him: it's Billy, who used to be in
the same street gang as Steve.

                    BILLY
          Steve? Steve McQueen?
                    (he turns to the
                    Duty Officer)
          You know who this is? This is
          the dirtbag who hightailed it
          and left me for dead — while two
          guys beat the crap outta me.

Steve shrugs his shoulders:

                    STEVE
          As I recall, 'cuz you were
          stealin' their hubcaps.

Billy glares distrustfully at Steve.

                    BILLY
          We, Steve. *We*.

                    DUTY OFFICER
          Ok, put it aside boys. You're
          marines now.

                                        CUT TO:

EXT. MILITARY LOT -- DAY

Steve and Billy, covered in grease, work on a tank.

> BILLY
> I guess it's the drive belt...

> STEVE
> No, no! It's the intake valve on
> the carburetor.

> BILLY
> You don't know what you're
> talking about—

> STEVE
> You're a moron. Just fix it like
> I told you.

> BILLY
> Blow me. I know what I'm doing.

> STEVE
> So do it yourself.

He steps away. Hands on hips, Steve scans the other
tanks.

After a moment—

> STEVE (CONT'D)
> Hey... what would happen if we
> souped up this baby?

> BILLY
> You gotta be kiddin' me.

> STEVE
> What else we gonna do on a
> Sunday?

                    BILLY
     How about we finish this.

                    STEVE
     You chicken?

                    BILLY
     You can't just, just go messing
     around with a Sherman tank—

                    STEVE
     Bawk! Bawk!

                    BILLY
     Fine. She's all yours.

Billy stands, making way for Steve, who grabs a
wrench and sets to work on the tank with gusto.

                    STEVE
     Watch the maestro.

                                        CUT TO:

EXT. FIELD -- DAY

A tank is in an empty field with soldiers crowded
around.

A solder is holding a stop-watch. Nearby, Billy
sullenly watches.

                    SOLDIER
     Everyone ready—?

Another soldier walks in front of the tank with a
checkered flag.

INT. TANK -- DAY

Inside the tank, Steve, giddy, stares at the start
flag.

> STEVE
>> C'mon, c'mon.
>>> (to his tank)
>> Don't let me down.

Steve's tank rumbles to life as he turns the
ignition. He's serious, focused.

EXT. FIELD -- DAY

The flag is lowered.

Click! The stop-watch starts.

Steve's off!

Soldiers cheer. Billy shakes his head.

INT. TANK -- DAY

Steve bounces in his seat, grinding the gears.

EXT. FIELD -- DAY

The tank races across the field while soldiers hoot
and holler.

A flock of birds, nesting, take to the sky to avoid
the on-rushing behemoth.

> SOLDIER
>> Go McQueen!

The tank thunders past a farmer's field. Cows watch.

INT. TANK -- DAY

                    STEVE
          Let's see what this baby can do!

He puts the pedal to the metal.

EXT. FIELD -- DAY

Steve's tank lurches forward.

                    SOLDIER
          Yeah!! Lookit 'em go!

EXT. FIELD -- DAY

Steve's tank suddenly bursts a gasket. Black smoke
spews from his vehicle.

INT. TANK -- DAY

                    STEVE
          Fuck!

EXT. FIELD -- DAY

Steve's tank careens out of control, veering to the
side. It slides into a steep ditch, before resting
among billowing fumes.

All the soldiers come running to help.

The soldiers pull Steve, covered in soot, from the
tank.

Once out, he laughs like a kid in a candy store.

                    STEVE
          Did you see that! She fish-
          tailed! I fuckin' fish-tailed a
          Sherman!

                                        CUT TO:

INT. MILITARY OFFICE -- DAY

Billy and Steve stand at attention before a
superior officer.

                    COLONEL
          Since when did this army become
          a joke?!!

The colonel addresses Billy:

                    COLONEL (CONT'D)
          What did you expect following
          this jar-head? McQueen's been
          busted down so many times it
          makes my head spin!

He turns to Steve.

                    COLONEL (CONT'D)
          As for you, one day, your life
          will depend on your fellow
          marines. Try and remember that.

                                        CUT TO:

INT. BOILER ROOM -- DAY

In a massive boiler room, Steve and Billy mop the
floor.

Steve glances at the ceiling. Orange tufts line the pipes and the fluff fills the air like dandruff.

                    STEVE
          What is that shit?

                    BILLY
          Asbestos.

                    STEVE
          At least this ain't the worst
          punishment detail I've been on.

Billy ignores him. Orange flakes rain down.

                                        CUT TO:

INT. BARRACKS -- DAY

Steve packs his duffel.

The staff Seargeant enters.

                    STAFF SEARGANT
          Take it easy, McQueen. Be back
          on base at oh-seven-hundred
          Monday morning.

                    STEVE
          Yes, sir

                                        CUT TO:

EXT. ARMY BASE -- DAY

Steve exits the base, duffel slung over his shoulder.

He saunters to the bus stop and lays in the grass, arms behind his head, staring up at the blue sky: freedom.

A bus stops.

INT. BUS -- DAY

Steve walks down the aisle, spotting a pretty blond.

He sits next to her.

She glances at his uniform. Steve smiles.

                                        CUT TO:

EXT. TOWN OF MYRTLE BEACH -- DAY

In downtown Myrtle beach, Steve walks arm-in-arm with Sue Ann. He's in full dress uniform while she's as proud as can be.

They pass the TV store. Steve tips his cap to his former boss.

                    STORE OWNER
          Good to see yah, Steve.

                                        CUT TO:

MONTAGE: Steve drinks a milkshake with Sue Ann in a soda shop, goes to the local fair, plays golf with her father, etc.

                                        FADE OUT:

EXT. BOARDWALK -- NIGHT

Steve walks with Sue Ann along the boardwalk. He
slips a whiskey flask from his uniform.

                    SUE ANN
          I don't like it when you drink,
          Steve.

                    STEVE
          Uh-huh.

He takes a swig anyway, when he spots an army jeep
across the street.

The MILITARY POLICE question someone stepping out
of a bar, pointing in his direction.

After another guzzle, Steve grabs Sue Ann brusquely
by the arm.

                    STEVE (CONT'D)
          C'mon. Let's go somewhere more
          private.

The jeep pulls alongside. The MPs get out.

                    MP
          PFC McQueen?

                    STEVE
          Gotta be lot of guys with that
          tag.

                    MP
          Private First Class Steven
          McQueen?

                    STEVE
          What of it?

                    SUE ANN
          Steve—?

                    MP
          You realize you have yet to
          report in?

                    STEVE
          Might be a little late.

                    MP
          How about two weeks late? Your
          leave pass was for the week-end.

                    SUE ANN
          Steve, what's he talking about,
          two weeks? You came by on Friday.

                    STEVE
          I dunno, he must be delusional.

                    MP
          Your boyfriend's AWOL.

                    SUE ANN
          Steve?

                    MP
          We've orders to bring him back
          with us.

                    STEVE
          Yeah, well, can't you see we're
          on a date?

                    MP
          Private, this would be a lot
          easier if—

One of the MPs takes Steve by the arm, separating
him from Sue Ann.

                    STEVE
          Don't touch her!

                    MP
          Just relax, soldier.

                    STEVE
          I told you to keep your hands
          off—

He slugs the MP. The others jump him.

                    SUE ANN
          Oh my god, Steve!

Steve brawls with the MPs.

                                        CUT TO:

INT. SOLITARY

Held by his elbows, Steve is led into solitary
confinement.

CLANG! The heavy cell door slams behind him.

                    COLONEL (V.O.)
          For failing to return to duty
          and fighting with fellow
          officers, Private Terrence
          Steven McQueen is hereby
          sentenced to solitary
          confinement.

Alone in his cell, Steve is defiant, pacing like a
caged tiger.

                                        CUT TO:

EXT. MANSION -- DAY

Sue Ann, tearful, hurries into a waiting taxicab.

                    SUE ANN
          Camp Lejeune.

                    TAXI DRIVER
          Are you serious lady? It ain't
          around the corner.

Reaching into her purse, Sue Ann flings at least a
hundred bucks at the driver.

                    SUE ANN
          Just take me there!

                                        CUT TO:

EXT. ENTRANCE TO CAMP LEJEUNE -- EVENING

The taxi pulls to a stop. Sue Ann hurries to the
entrance.

INT. CAMP LEJEUNE RECEPTION -- EVENING

Calming her nerves, Sue Ann approaches the
receptionist.

                    SUE ANN
          I'm here to see Steve McQueen.

The receptionist glances at a clipboard.

                    RECEPTIONIST
          I'm sorry, but no one's allowed—

                    SUE ANN
          I haven't heard anything in over
          a month! Has something happened
          to him?

                    RECEPTIONIST
          Just a minute, ma'am.

The receptionist signals another officer, who scans
the clipboard.

                    OFFICER
          Private McQueen is alright miss,
          but he's got ten more days to go.

                    SUE ANN
          I don't understand. Ten more
          days for what?

                    OFFICER
          He's been sentenced to solitary
          confinement for forty-one days.

Sue Ann soaks in the news.

                                        CUT TO:

INT. SOLITARY

Steve sits on his haunches in the gloomy cell.

He's a mess, his face covered in stubble.

He glances at the ceiling.

The voices are like ghosts, haunting and distant:

                    LILLIAN (V.O.)
          You'll never escape from here!

The voice echoes. Steve tries to shake it away, to no avail.

                                    CUT TO:

EXT. THOMSON FARMSTEAD -- DAY

Tall grass sways in the breeze by the Thomson farmstead, Steve's childhood home.

                    FRANK GRAVES (V.O.)
          You could be somebody special...

INT. SOLITARY

Steve covers his ears. And sobs.

                    STEVE
          Father...

He breaks into tears.

INT. SOLITARY

The door opens.

Light falls on Steve. He shades his eyes.

Rebuffing offers of assistance, he shakily walks out on his own.

                                    FADE OUT:

INT. ARMY FILES DEPARTMENT -- DAY

Steve pushes a mail cart into the file department. The clerk passes him a clipboard for his signature.

                    ARMY CLERK
          Private McQueen?

                    STEVE
          Yeah.

                    ARMY CLERK
          Name rings a bell.

                    STEVE
          Uh-huh.

                    ARMY CLERK
          Pretty sure I saw another
          McQueen in the files, maybe
          related? Marine. A flyer.

                    STEVE
          You mean a pilot?

                    ARMY CLERK
          That's right. Any in your
          family?

                    STEVE
          My father was a pilot.

                    ARMY CLERK
          Just a sec.

The clerk rummages.

                    ARMY CLERK (CONT'D)
          Damn, I can't find it now. This
          place is such a mess. I got a
          ton of shit to get to.

                    STEVE
          I can look, if you don't mind.

                    ARMY CLERK
        Ok, when you're off duty, come
        on by.

                                        CUT TO:

INT. ARMY FILES DEPARTMENT -- LATER

A stack of files is spread on a desk. Steve rifles
through the "M's" while absently snapping Red's
Zippo open and shut.

Click — open.

Clack — closed.

                                    DISSOLVE TO:

INT. ARMY FILES DEPARTMENT -- LATER

Steve continues to rummage, bleary eyed. The files
in front of him are in complete disorder.

He rubs his cheeks stifling a yawn. Still nothing.

                                    DISSOLVE TO:

INT. ARMY FILES DEPARTMENT -- LATER

Disappointed, Steve flicks off the light switch,
closing the door.

His search has been fruitless.

                                        FADE OUT:

EXT. ARCTIC RIVER -- DAY

An inflatable army boat purrs across impenetrable
water.

The surrounding landscape is barren, speckled with snow and ice. A subtitle reads: **Northern Labrador.**

Sitting at the front of the boat, Steve dreamily watches the shore float past.

>   STEVE
>   A'right. Cut it.

His breath condenses in the frigid air.

The soldier driving the boat turns off the engine.

EXT. ARCTIC BEACH / OUTPOST -- DAY

They float onto the grey beach.

In front of them are a few sparse tents: a northern training outpost.

Steve and the others drag the boat onto the beach.

>   LEUTENANT
>   Welcome to the frozen armpit of
>   the world, gents.

Steve salutes.

>   STEVE
>   Sir. The transports 're about 10
>   minutes behind.

>   LEUTENANT
>   Alright Private. Get yourself
>   some grub.

EXT. TRANSPORT BOAT -- DAY

Two transports ferry tanks to the training outpost.

Billy stands with another soldier in the prow.

>   BILLY
> They expect us to fight a war up
> here?

>   SOLDIER
> I friggin' hate arctic exercises.

>   CAPTAIN
> Ready the lead tank to
> disembark!

>   BILLY
> Yes, sir!

Billy, with his crewmen, climbs into the tank.

INT. TANK -- DAY

Billy settles into the driver's seat.

The gunner, above him, closes the hatch, locking it.

EXT. ARCTIC RIVER -- DAY

The transports glide along still water.

EXT. UNDERWATER -- DAY

An underwater shot reveals the hull of the
transport slicing through the river...

...Where ahead lies a jagged outcropping, just beneath the surface.

EXT. ARCTIC BEACH / OUTPOST -- DAY

Steve emerges from a tent. He taps his ear, as if hearing something out of the ordinary.

It's the sound of the boat's engine, underwater.

EXT. UNDERWATER -- DAY

The transport bears down on the outcropping.

EXT. ARCTIC BEACH / OUTPOST -- DAY

Steve stares at the water.

The strangely pitched frequency gets louder, buzzing in his ear.

EXT. TRANSPORT BOAT -- DAY

BAM!

The transport rocks violently. Crates slide to the edge of the deck.

INT. TANK -- DAY

Inside the tank, Billy and his crew are rattled, leaning at an extreme angle.

                    BILLY
        What the hell was that?! Are we
        on the beach?!

                    GUNNER
            I don't think so—

A terrible grinding noise, like tearing metal, cuts
them off.

The tank starts to move.

EXT. ARCTIC BEACH / OUTPOST -- DAY

The transport flounders, one half sinking into the
water, the other raised in the air.

Steve, already alert, jumps into the inflatable
boat while the other soldiers, riveted, gawk at the
accident.

EXT. ARCTIC RIVER -- DAY

Steve drives the boat all-out toward the transport.

EXT. TRANSPORT BOAT -- DAY

With a gut wrenching screech, the tank slides
across the deck...

...Careening over the side.

INT. TANK -- DAY

The tank compartment spins, throwing Billy around
like a rag doll.

INT. UNDERWATER -- DAY

Underwater, the tank breaks through the surface!

INT. ARCTIC RIVER -- DAY

The transport sinks with men quickly abandoning it.
The transport behind is fast approaching.

Steve steers the inflatable between the two vessels,
waving his arms.

                    STEVE
          Veer off!!! Veer off!!! It's too
          shallow!

INT. TANK -- DAY

The gunner attempts to open the hatch.

                    GUNNER
          It's jammed!

Water is gushing in. Billy slides out of his seat.

He checks the soldier next to him who's lying prone.
Blood pours from his temple. Billy takes his pulse.

Nothing.

                    BILLY
          Get it open, dammit!

EXT. ARCTIC RIVER -- DAY

The tank rocks gently in the water, lapped by
waves... sliding completely beneath the surface.

Steve, meanwhile, slows his boat next to the second transport.

> STEVE
> The 1st transport's going under!
> Pull back and get some boats in
> the water! We need help here!

The Captain of the transport nods and issues rapid-fire instructions to his men.

Steve speeds ahead.

INT. TANK -- DAY

The tank is flooding with water. It's up to their waists.

The two men continue to heave on the hatch.

> BILLY
> Goddamn!

EXT. ARCTIC RIVER -- DAY

Steve zooms past the transport to where he saw the tank go down. He cups his hands to men in another dinghy:

> STEVE
> What's the situation? I saw a
> tank go down.

> SOLDIER
> The crew was inside!

Steve cuts the engine. He can't see anything beneath the dark water.

Stillness.

The lapping of waves.

Then Steve leaps into the water.

EXT. UNDERWATER -- DAY

And shoots through the surface.

He dives, down, down...

Steve sees the army tank silently sink to the
bottom, eerily out of place on the riverbed.

INT. TANK -- DAY

The water is up to Billy's neck.

                    GUNNER
          What the fuck do we do?

EXT. ARCTIC RIVER -- DAY

Steve breaks the surface, gasping for breath,
before diving back down...

EXT. UNDERWATER -- DAY

Steve grabs onto the tank's hatch.

INT. TANK -- DAY

Inside the tank, they hear a metal clang.

> BILLY
> C'mon, push! Push!

They heave on the hatch. Water rains down on them.

EXT. UNDERWATER -- DAY

Steve struggles, bubbles flowing from his lips.

He gasps —

— out of breath.

And pulls!

INT. TANK -- DAY

The hatch opens.

EXT. UNDERWATER -- DAY

Steve swims for the surface with Billy and the gunner following in his wake.

EXT. TRANSPORT BOAT -- DAY

Steve is pulled aboard the second transport.

Teeth chattering, someone throws a blanket over him. He pushes back the medic who's come to check on him.

> STEVE
> It's ok. I'm alright.

Billy pushes through the throng.

Solemnly, he sticks out his hand:

                    BILLY
          Thank you.

They grip hands.

Other soldiers pat Steve on the back.

Some clap.

Standing in a circle of soldiers and overwrought
with emotion, Steve struggles not to tear up.

Instead, he laughs.

FADE TO BLACK.

All that's heard is Steve's laughter.

EXT. HARBOR -- DAY

A beautiful sunlit day.

A splendid yacht, the *Sequoia*, sails into harbor.

EXT. DECK OF THE SEQUOIA -- DAY

Steve is on deck in a spotless uniform, standing
guard next to the cabin.

A man in an elegant suit exits. He leans on the
railing.

                    TRUMAN
          Corporal?

                    STEVE
          We're putting into harbor, sir.

The man nods, thoughtful. He pulls out a cigar then searches for matches, but comes up short.

                    TRUMAN
          Sorry, Corporal, but could you—?

Steve reaches into his jacket. He takes out his Zippo with the word "Red" engraved on it.

                    STEVE
          Mr. President—

Steve lights the President's cigar.

                    ADVISOR (O.S.)
          President Truman?

The President joins his advisors while Steve smiles inwardly.

EXT. HARBOR -- DAY

The yacht sails into the morning sunshine.

                              FADE TO WHITE:

EXT. MANSION (GARDEN LAWN) -- NIGHT

A long buffet table has been laid out in an exquisite garden.

The leaders of the county are present, dressed in their finest. A five piece band plays on the patio.

Steve, in full military uniform —medal on his chest— emerges from the back entrance, arm-in-arm with Sue Ann.

PERRY
Steve! Sue Ann!

He waves them over.

PERRY (CONT'D)
You look beautiful darling...
Steve, I want you to know I have
special plans for you.

STEVE
Sir?

PERRY
You make Sue Ann happy and
you're going to make our family
very proud.

SUE ANN
Oh, daddy! Steve, I bet my
father's boring you.

PERRY
Alright, honey. We'll talk some
more later, Steve.

Sue Ann leads Steve down a garden path.

STEVE
Sue Ann, what's your father
talking about? What special
plan?

SUE ANN
Don't be paranoid Steve. A job.

STEVE
What job?

                        SUE ANN
        Six figures with your own office.
        You'll have to learn the ropes,
        of course.

Steve watches her, but he's not listening.

Her voice and the garden party music *fades away*.

He can't bear the thought of others controlling his
every movement.

                    SUE ANN (CONT'D)
        Steve? Is everything alright?

                        STEVE
        Sure.

They continue to stroll, silently, arm-in-arm.

                    STEVE (CONT'D)
        Drink?

                        SUE ANN
        Steve—

                        STEVE
        To celebrate.

She smiles and lets go of his arm. Sue Ann wanders
to some friends while Steve heads for the open bar.

He pours himself a drink, even as Sue Ann chats
happily.

He sips from a champagne glass, watching Sue Ann.
He stares at her and the other guests, laughing,
drinking, effecting to be fancy and polished...
Steve knows he'll never fit in. He doesn't belong
to this world.

At last, Sue Ann notices Steve hasn't returned.

She turns around, glancing at the bar, but Steve's nowhere to be seen.

                                        FADE OUT:

EXT. LOGGING ROAD -- MORNING

In the morning, Steve walks along a logging road in his jeans and t-shirt.

A truck rumbles up. Steve turns, sticking out his thumb.

The truck stops.

Steve gets in.

                                        FADE OUT:

EXT. RACE TRACK -- DAY

Motorbikes roar round a track.

Crowds press behind a wooden fence, cheering on the amateur riders.

A subtitle reads: **Coney Island, 1951.**

Soaring through a cloud of dust, Steve appears, shirt open, riding a Harley.

He's determined, pushing his bike to its limits.

Suddenly, another bike cuts him off and Steve takes a spill.

Before coming to a full stop, he picks up his bike, hopping back on.

Steve presses through the pack... edging up on the
leader.

                                              CUT TO:

INT. BAR -- DAY

Steve hops on a bar stool.

                    STEVE
          Gimme a cheeseburger and some
          pie, with a Coors to wash it
          down.

                    BARMAN
          Sorry desperado. Kitchen's
          closed.

Steve sees that other people are eating.

                    STEVE
          What's the deal?

The barman grabs a tab pinned to a post.

                    BARMAN
          Remember this?

                    STEVE
          A'right, a'right. Quit twisting
          my melon.

Steve pulls a wad of bills from his jeans, counting
out the money. The barman is surprised to see Steve
is loaded.

                                              CUT TO:

INT. BAR -- MOMENTS LATER

Steve wolfs down his burger with one hand, holding
a slab of pie in the other.

He's oblivious to the world—

—While a woman sitting at a nearby table watches
him.

She's in her mid-thirties, zonked out on alcohol
with matted hair.

Sensing her gaze, Steve casts a suspicious eye.

                    JULLIAN
          Tell me you don't know me,
          Steven.

He stares at his mother for a long moment, before
turning back to his beer.

                    STEVE
          Drop dead.

Jullian attempts to stand, but she's drunk.

She barely steadies herself on a chair.

                    JULLIAN
          For god's sake, at least give me
          your hand and help me out of
          here.

                                        CUT TO:

EXT. BAR -- DAY

Steve tenderly helps his mother outside. He
rummages in his pockets and hands her some money.

She looks at it, before reluctantly accepting the cash.

Standing on the curb of Broadway, they stare at each other: there's too much to say, so they say nothing.

Jullian nods her head, wobbling away.

Steve watches her hunched back, before walking in the opposite direction.

                                        FADE OUT:

INT. APARTMENT BUILDING STAIRWELL -- DAY

Steve bounds up the stairs—

INT. STEVE'S APARTMENT -- DAY

And enters a dingy apartment. On a mattress in the corner is a half-naked girl: his latest conquest.

He holds up the prize money, forcing a smile.

                    STEVE
          This month's rent.

                    GIRL
          You gotta find something else
          Steve. It's too dangerous. You
          can't win races forever.

                    STEVE
          Why not?

She puts her arms around him.

                    GIRL
You've already conned your way
round the world. Come to my
acting class. I think you'd be
good.

                    STEVE
Acting's not somethin' for a
grown man to be doing.

                    GIRL
What's that supposed to mean?

                    STEVE
It's candy ass. Acting's hip for
a few laughs and to meet chicks—

                    GIRL
—like me?

                    STEVE
Whatever you say...

                    GIRL
Don't think I don't know you've
seen other girls.

                    STEVE
I've been thinking of learnin' a
trade. Maybe lay tile in Spain.

                    GIRL
Why not the French Riviera?
You're such a dreamer.

                                        CUT TO:

EXT. GREENWICH VILLAGE -- DAY

Steve, without a shirt, drives his girlfriend
through the streets of New York on his Harley.

They roar through Greenwich village past beatniks,
Bohemians and bums.

His girlfriend prattles into his ear, over the
wind:

> GIRL
> You hafta do something with your
> life, Steve. Go back to school...

> STEVE
> I ain't got dough for school.

> GIRL
> You were in the marines, baby.
> The G.I. bill. I'm serious.

She gets off in front of a building with a sign
over the door: Sanford Meisner's Neighborhood
Playhouse.

> STEVE
> Alright, I'll see you later.

> GIRL
> Think about it.

Steve watches her go inside.

He stares at the sign for a long moment,
contemplating his future.

He pulls out a cigar, sticking it in his mouth.

Steve reaches into his jeans and pulls out the
Zippo with "Red" engraved on it.

He lights his cigar and lets out a thoughtful puff
of smoke.

                                        CUT TO:

INT / EXT. TAXI GARAGE -- DAY

A grizzled mechanic is underneath a yellow taxicab.
He bangs his head.

                    MECHANIC
          Christ—

Steve, standing by the open garage, is watching.

                    STEVE
          Hey, need a hand with that?

                    MECHANIC
          Kid — you can fix it, you can
          drive it.

                                        CUT TO:

EXT. NEW YORK STREETS -- DAY

Steve drives the taxi through New York traffic.

INT. TAXICAB -- DAY

Through the rear view mirror, Steve glances at a
wealthy couple in the back seat.

                    LADY
              (imitating a deep,
              masculine voice)
          Stella...! Stella...!
              (giggling)
          My goodness he was fabulous.

                    BANK MAN
          What's he got that I don't?

> LADY
> (laughing)
> Everything! Hah! I'd give up my
> liver to spend five minutes with
> a man like that!

The lady notices Steve watching her in the mirror:
a sly smile crosses her lips. Steve pulls to the
curb.

> STEVE
> Here we are folks.

The man counts out the fare while the lady leans
over the seat, addressing Steve.

> LADY
> Have you seen Brando? I mean
> have you? He's divine.

> BANK MAN
> Ok, shut your yapper and get out.
> Here you go, kid.

Steve shares an impetuous, parting glance with the
lady.

> CUT TO:

INT. TAXICAB -- NIGHT

Alone, Steve drives, thoughtful. He watches New
York pass by.

Through the window, he spots a marquee: A STREETCAR
NAMED DESIRE.

Throngs are lined up to see the movie.

EXT. NEW YORK STREET CORNER (PHONE BOOTH) --
NIGHT

Steve's cab is parked next to a phone booth. He's
inside, dialing, glancing at the paper given to him
by his girlfriend.

The clamor of the city nearly drowns him out:

> STEVE
> Yeah, I wanna audition.

                                        CUT TO:

INT. STEVE'S APARTMENT -- DAY

The sun is harsh and bright through the apartment
window.

Steve's bare-chested, in jeans.

In his hand is a crumpled script, pages of which
are littered on the floor.

He guzzles from a beer, muttering lines of text
while absently grabbing his father's lighter.

Flicking it, Steve paces.

He glances at the page.

CLICK

CLACK

Steve speaks his lines... but all that's heard is
the city.

Tearing off a sheet, Steve memorizes another line —
defiantly crumpling the paper into a ball.

While reciting, Steve recalls his mother's voice:

> JULLIAN (V.O.)
> It was my fault. When I get to
> drinkin'... Berri's a good man
> and discipline ain't a bad thing.

                                    FLASH CUT TO:

INT. MOVIE PALACE -- DAY

Sitting in the darkness of a movie theater, Jullian
studies Steve carefully.

> STEVE (V.O.)
> What was my father like?

Jullian stares at him, not sure what to answer...

                                    FLASH CUT BACK TO:

INT. STEVE'S APARTMENT -- DAY

Steve holds up another sheet — and lights it. While
staring at the flame, he recites. As before, no
sound comes from his mouth.

Instead, the cacophony of the city fades into the
sound of wind rustling through tall grass: the
sounds of Steve's youth.

His words remain inaudible...

The flame brightens.

CUT TO BLACK

                                            END

ABOUT THE AUTHOR

D.R. SCHOEL is an award winning writer and filmmaker who has worked for nearly twenty years with the Inuit of the Arctic on many television documentaries. He also collaborated with Chad McQueen (son of movie icon Steve McQueen) on an un-produced project for Netflix, and wrote the feature film "Adam's Wall", a Jewish-Arab love story, released globally. He directed the short film "The Fantastic Bus" which was presented at Cannes and, among other honors, won a Canadian Screen Award (the equivalent of the Canadian Oscars) for "Sol", about an Inuit circus performer who died in RCMP custody, which he co-wrote with Marie-Hélène Cousineau.

Made in the USA
Columbia, SC
25 October 2020